New Day

Edited by Naomi Starkey

May–August 2014

New Daylight © BRF 2014

The Bible Reading Fellowship
15 The Chambers, Vineyard, Abingdon OX14 3FE
Tel: 01865 319700; Fax: 01865 319701
E-mail: enquiries@brf.org.uk; Website: www.brf.org.uk

ISBN 978 0 85746 035 6

Distributed in Australia by Mediacom Education Inc., PO Box 610, Unley, SA 5061.
Tel: 1800 811 311; Fax: 08 8297 8719;
E-mail: admin@mediacom.org.au
Available also from all good Christian bookshops in Australia.
For individual and group subscriptions in Australia:
Mrs Rosemary Morrall, PO Box W35, Wanniassa, ACT 2903.

Distributed in New Zealand by Scripture Union Wholesale, PO Box 760, Wellington
Tel: 04 385 0421; Fax: 04 384 3990; E-mail: suwholesale@clear.net.nz

Publications distributed to more than 60 countries

Suggestions for using *New Daylight*

Find a regular time and place, if possible, where you can read and pray undisturbed. Before you begin, take time to be still and perhaps use the BRF prayer. Then read the Bible passage slowly (try reading it aloud if you find it over-familiar), followed by the comment. You can also use *New Daylight* for group study and discussion, if you prefer.

The prayer or point for reflection can be a starting point for your own meditation and prayer. Many people like to keep a journal to record their thoughts about a Bible passage and items for prayer. In *New Daylight* we also note the Sundays and some special festivals from the Church calendar, to keep in step with the Christian year.

New Daylight and the Bible

New Daylight contributors use a range of Bible versions, and you will find a list of the versions used opposite, on page 2. You are welcome to use your own preferred version alongside the passage printed in the notes, and this can be particularly helpful if the Bible text has been abridged.

New Daylight affirms that the whole of the Bible is God's revelation to us, and we should read, reflect on and learn from every part of both Old and New Testaments. Usually the printed comment presents a straight-forward 'thought for the day', but sometimes it may also raise questions rather than simply providing answers, as we wrestle with some of the more difficult passages of Scripture.

New Daylight *is also available in a deluxe edition (larger format). Check out your local Christian bookshop or contact the BRF office, who can also give more details about a cassette version for the visually impaired. For a Braille edition, contact St John's Guild, 8 St Raphael's Court, Avenue Road, St Albans, AL1 3EH.*

Writers in this issue

David Winter is retired from parish ministry. An honorary Canon of Christ Church, Oxford, he is well known as a writer and broadcaster. His most recent book for BRF is *At the End of the Day*.

Veronica Zundel is an Oxford graduate, writer and journalist. She lives with her husband and son in North London, where they belong to the Mennonite Church.

Penelope Wilcock writes Christian fiction, pastoral theology and Bible study. Her books include 'The Hawk & the Dove' series, *Spiritual Care of Dying and Bereaved People*, *100 Stand-Alone Bible Studies* and *Learning To Let Go*. She blogs at http://kindredofthequietway.blogspot.co.uk.

Steve Aisthorpe lives in Scotland with his wife and two sons. He is a Development Officer for the Church of Scotland, encouraging mission and discipleship throughout the Highlands and Islands. He was previously Executive Director of the International Nepal Fellowship.

Tony Horsfall is a freelance trainer and retreat leader based in Yorkshire, with his own ministry, Charis Training. He is an elder of Ackworth Community Church and has written several books for BRF, including *Working from a Place of Rest* and *Servant Ministry*.

Stephen Rand is a writer and speaker who worked with Tearfund for many years, and then Open Doors, travelling widely. He now helps lead Fresh Streams—a largely Baptist church leaders' network. He and his wife Susan live in Oxfordshire, not too far from their grandchildren.

Bob Mayo is a vicar in Shepherds Bush. He is married, is the chaplain at QPR and can be seen in the parks of west London walking his two dachshund dogs. He is a keen runner and ran his twelfth marathon in Bethlehem in order to bring attention to the situation in the Middle East.

Andrew Jones is Archdeacon of Meirionnydd in the Diocese of Bangor. He has written *Pilgrimage: the journey to remembering our story* for BRF and is writing *Mary: a Gospel witness to transfiguration and liberation*.

Liz Hoare is tutor in prayer and pastoral studies at Wycliffe Hall Oxford. A historian by training, she has a special interest in Celtic and desert spiritualities and a deep commitment to accompanying people in prayer. She is married to Toddy, an ordained Anglican priest and sculptor, and they have one son.

Naomi Starkey writes...

Writing the editor's letter is one of the later stages of putting together an issue of New Daylight. The readings have been commissioned and edited, the pages designed and checked by both the copy-editor and proofreader, the cover image chosen and cover wording agreed. It is time for the editor to review the issue as a whole and reflect on what to highlight for the benefit of readers.

In this issue a number of contributors have provided readings that turn out to link in some way to the theme of being chosen to do God's work and being open to God's timing. Steve Aisthorpe writes another in our series of 'Bible stories rediscovered', which aims to take a fresh look at episodes we may not have considered since encountering them (and perhaps colouring in a picture) at Sunday school. This time the focus is on Gideon, an unlikely figure to emerge as a strong leader during a period of great uncertainty for Israel.

At the end of June, the church remembers the apostles Peter and Paul, and around that time Tony Horsfall's readings explore how God calls us to ministry just as we are, even if we feel we fall far short of anything approaching pioneer or evangelist material. Meanwhile, in August (with the feast of the Transfiguration on 6 August) Andrew Jones considers the liberating and transfiguring power of God's grace and how it can be released to bless our lives.

I am pleased to welcome two new contributors: Bob Mayo, who writes on the major biblical concept of 'the Day of the Lord', and Penelope Wilcock, whose readings on 'Building God's kingdom on earth' fall in with the feasts of Ascension and Pentecost. It is good, too, to begin a new series in which contributors share the Bible passages that have come to mean most to them. David Winter's readings on 'My favourite Scriptures' open this issue.

In this 25th anniversary year of New Daylight, I would ask for your prayers for the BRF team as we look back and give thanks for God's gracious guidance—and as we look forward in planning Bible reading and other resources for the future.

The BRF Prayer

Almighty God,
you have taught us that your word is a lamp for our feet
and a light for our path. Help us, and all who prayerfully
read your word, to deepen our fellowship with you
and with each other through your love.
And in so doing may we come to know you more fully,
love you more truly, and follow more faithfully
in the steps of your son Jesus Christ, who lives and reigns
with you and the Holy Spirit, one God for evermore.
Amen

My favourite scriptures

It is very generous of our editor to offer me the chance to choose my favourite readings! In one way it is easy, because there are plenty to choose from, but for the same reason it is difficult. I am spoilt for choice.

In the event, I have tried to choose passages that, for me, represent great moments of revelation. If the Bible is all about God revealing his truth and our gradual comprehension of his purposes, then these readings represent my personal file of 'eureka' moments. I think every serious reader of the Bible recognises that there are occasions when something hitherto obscure or complicated becomes utterly clear—the truth breaks through like the rising sun in the morning. Each of these readings has, at different times, done precisely that for me.

I have started with Exodus (Moses at the burning bush) and ended with Revelation (the new Jerusalem). In between, I invite you to travel with me through several key moments in the unfolding story of God and the human race—the dedication of the temple, the spirituality of the Psalms, great words of hope from Isaiah, the voice of Jesus himself in the Gospels, Paul writing to new Christians in the city of Colosse and then the final glorious vision of the new Jerusalem. My readings not only cover over a thousand years of history but also great moments when there was some advance in God's revelation of his nature and character and humans' understanding of his ways.

The remarkable thing to me is that, in one sense, they all speak with the same voice. Moses at the burning bush on the slopes of Sinai met exactly the same God as the Christians in Colosse gathering centuries later on a Sunday evening for fellowship and prayer—and the very same God as you and I meet in prayer and worship today. There is only one God, whose name is YHWH, the Eternal One, and the authentic voice of scripture is his. I hope that in these 'favourite passages' of mine you will find, as I have, a way of hearing that voice with clarity, beauty and power.

David Winter

The God who hears our cry

Then the Lord said, '… The cry of the Israelites has now come to me; I have also seen how the Egyptians oppress them. So come, I will send you to Pharaoh to bring my people, the Israelites, out of Egypt.' But Moses said to God, 'Who am I that I should go to Pharaoh, and bring the Israelites out of Egypt?' He said, 'I will be with you…' But Moses said to God, 'If I come to the Israelites and say to them, "The God of your ancestors has sent me to you", and they ask me, "What is his name?" what shall I say to them?' God said to Moses, 'I AM WHO I AM.'

Moses fled from Egypt after murdering a man (Exodus 2:11–15) and then married the daughter of a Midianite priest. He has led the family flock to the foothills of Mount Sinai, where his eye is caught by a burning bush. He draws near and finds that he is engaged in a unique encounter with God, a 'conversation' (whether aloud or in the private depths of his consciousness) that is to change his life. Because of its significance in the whole story of the Bible, I have chosen it as the first of this selection of 'favourite passages'.

Moses had left his fellow Hebrews still in slavery in Egypt. He knew that they had cried to God for deliverance, so he would have been encouraged to learn that the Lord had, in fact, heard their prayers. What he found less encouraging was the discovery that he was to be the human agent of their rescue. God was sending him back to Egypt.

His first objection is fundamental: 'If I say that God has sent me, and they ask his name, what shall I say?' In response, the Lord revealed his true identity as being not 'the God of Abraham, Isaac and Jacob' but the awesome eternal Creator whose name is YHWH, which is believed to be a form of the Hebrew present tense, 'I am'. God, then, simply exists. He has no beginning, no ending. He just *is*! It was I AM who was sending Moses to Pharaoh.

Reflection
The eternal Creator, the one who 'is', hears our cries!

DAVID WINTER

1 KINGS 8:27–30 (NRSV)

Place and prayer

'But will God indeed dwell on the earth? Even heaven and the highest heaven cannot contain you, much less this house that I have built! Regard your servant's prayer and his plea, O Lord my God, heeding the cry and the prayer that your servant prays to you today; that your eyes may be open night and day toward this house, the place of which you said, "My name shall be there," that you may heed the prayer that your servant prays toward this place. Hear the plea of your servant and of your people Israel when they pray toward this place; O hear in heaven your dwelling place; heed and forgive.'

Forty years ago there was a religious broadcasting series on Radio 3 called *The Long Search*, which told the story of a 'double' search: God for us and us for God. In that search, which has lasted the whole duration of human experience, yesterday's reading recorded a crucial moment: the revealing of God as the 'I AM', the eternal One. Today's reading—from King Solomon's prayer at the consecration of the first great temple in Jerusalem—tells of another. God does not live in holy places; he is not to be found in the sun or the moon, on a mountain top or a sacred grove—or even in a beautiful temple. We may be more aware of God in certain places, which therefore become holy to us, but he is present everywhere.

Of course, when we gather to worship him or to pray, we become more aware of that presence. Jesus promised that 'where two or three are gathered in my name, I am there among them' (Matthew 18:20). It is the gathering that is holy, however, not the building in which the gathering takes place. God's holy 'Name' is there because his people have gathered to recognise it and honour him. It could be a place of prayer by the river (Acts 16:13) or a great cathedral, a kitchen prayer meeting or choral evensong. It is not the place that matters, but his presence.

Reflection
'The glory of the Lord filled the house of the Lord' (1 Kings 8:11).
No God, no glory!

DAVID WINTER

PSALM 62:1–2, 7–12 (NRSV, ABRIDGED)

Waiting on God

For God alone my soul waits in silence; from him comes my salvation. He alone is my rock and my salvation, my fortress; I shall
never be shaken... On God rests my deliverance and my honour;
my mighty rock, my refuge is in God. Trust in him at all times, O
people; pour out your heart before him; God is a refuge for us.
Those of low estate are but a breath, those of high estate are a
delusion; in the balances they go up; they are together lighter than
a breath... If riches increase, do not set your heart on them. Once
God has spoken; twice have I heard this: that power belongs to
God, and steadfast love belongs to you, O Lord. For you repay to
all according to their work.

This is a wonderful psalm to use at the start of a Quiet Day or, indeed,
as a reflection before morning or evening prayer. Its key idea is 'alone'—
'for God alone my soul waits in silence' (v. 1). The psalmist then sets
God's resilient qualities alongside the alternatives. God is my rock, my
salvation, my fortress, my refuge. He is the source of both power and
'steadfast love'. He is my 'deliverance' (from evil) and my 'honour' (the
one who gives me worth). Besides all that, of what enduring value are
riches and reputation? They are fleeting and unreliable, whereas the
Lord is utterly trustworthy.

This is the God for whom we 'wait in silence'. 'Waiting' is a common
theme in the Psalms—not the exasperating 'waiting' for a bus that never
comes or a phone which never rings, but 'waiting' for the dependable
purposes of God to be fulfilled. Like the watchmen on the walls of the
city (Psalm 130:5–6), gazing to the east to catch the first glimpse of the
rising sun and wake the residents for the new day, we 'wait' for what we
know is assured—the loving purposes of a faithful God.

Reflection

*Not always, but certainly sometimes, our spiritual priority must be this
sense of 'isolation' with God. 'For God alone my soul waits in silence'
(Psalm 62:1).*

DAVID WINTER

A mother's prayer

O Lord, my heart is not lifted up, my eyes are not raised too high; I do not occupy myself with things too great and too marvellous for me. But I have calmed and quieted my soul, like a weaned child with its mother; my soul is like the weaned child that is with me. O Israel, hope in the Lord from this time on and for evermore.

I have often read this psalm to groups and asked them if anything strikes them about its author. It usually takes quite a lot of prodding to provoke what seems to me the obvious response: it is written by a woman. The very idea that a woman might write one of the 'psalms of David' strikes some as unthinkable, even though, over recent centuries, women have written many much-loved hymns. (Incidentally, the 'psalms of David' is not the same thing as 'David's psalms', any more than a Wesleyan hymnbook only includes hymns by Charles Wesley!)

Anyone taking this psalm at face value would surely assume that it was by a woman—the beautiful image of 'the weaned child that is with me' seems to clinch the case. Not only that but also, in the context of an intensely patriarchal society, where women were expected to attend to the home and children and leave weightier matters to the male head of the family, this psalm breathes a genuine and unforced humility that feeds the human spirit, male or female: 'I do not occupy myself with things too great or too marvellous for me.' Perhaps it takes a mother with her young child to appreciate fully what is truly important and what is not. To fix our eyes on simple things, to not be preoccupied with the 'great and marvellous', can indeed 'calm and quieten the soul'.

Anyone who has watched a baby at its mother's breast or seen the satisfaction on its face when it is finally full of warm milk will recognise the power of the metaphor. We are hungry for love, for truth, for peace of mind. Our hearts long for fullness but the Lord himself is the only one in whom all our hungers are satisfied.

Reflection

'Like newborn infants, long for the pure, spiritual milk' (1 Peter 2:2).

True comfort

Comfort, O comfort my people, says your God. Speak tenderly to Jerusalem, and cry to her that she has served her term, that her penalty is paid, that she has received from the Lord's hand double for all her sins. A voice cries out: 'In the wilderness prepare the way of the Lord, make straight in the desert a highway for our God. Every valley shall be lifted up, and every mountain and hill be made low; the uneven ground shall become level, and the rough places a plain. Then the glory of the Lord shall be revealed, and all people shall see it together, for the mouth of the Lord has spoken.'

This is a favourite passage of mine for two reasons. The first is that it sings in my head, thanks to Handel's beautiful arrangement of these words in his *Messiah*! The second is that it is a wonderful treatment of the whole concept of 'comfort'.

The people of Judah had suffered for 60 years at the hands of their Babylonian conquerors. The temple of God had been ransacked, their harvests had been plundered, their fellow Jews enslaved in Babylon and, every day, to make it worse, the prophet Isaiah outside the temple ruins would cry, 'Woe!' It was all their fault. It was their sin and disobedience that had brought about the disaster.

Yet, one day, 60 years after the Babylonians first came, a prophet—another 'Isaiah'—had a new message. It was no longer 'Woe', but—unbelievably—'Comfort'. They had paid the price for their sins. Deliverance was at hand, but they would have to be prepared for it. The 'rough places' must be made smooth; the crooked road through the desert of disobedience must be made straight. When this had been done, God's glory would be revealed and, in place of his judgment, they would know his tender love and compassion once again. There, in a nutshell, is the whole theology of judgment, repentance and forgiveness.

Reflection

What was true in the sixth century BC is still true for us today. The difference is, the price of our sin has been paid already.

DAVID WINTER

MATTHEW 11:27–30 (NRSV)

The shared burden

[Jesus said] 'All things have been handed over to me by my Father; and no one knows the Son except the Father, and no one knows the Father except the Son and anyone to whom the Son chooses to reveal him. Come to me, all you that are weary and are carrying heavy burdens, and I will give you rest. Take my yoke upon you, and learn from me; for I am gentle and humble in heart, and you will find rest for your souls. For my yoke is easy, and my burden is light.'

This one was a simple choice. Like many Bible readers, for me this is supremely one of the 'precious and very great promises' of God (2 Peter 1:4). The direct invitation of Jesus is about as unambiguous as you can get. 'Come to me, all you that are weary and are carrying heavy burdens, and I will give you rest' (Matthew 11:28). Our individual burdens and causes of weariness may vary, but the promise stands.

It is all the stronger for what precedes it. The one who offers to share our burdens is none other than the unique Son, the one who is 'close to the Father's heart' (John 1:18). To 'take his yoke' is to invite him to share our burdens, like the partner ox pulling a plough, but he is much the stronger ox, gentle and humble. Despite being gentle, he is able to carry not only our burden but also the burden of the whole world's sin and failure. With him beside us, what had seemed unbearable becomes light.

The clue to this blessing is both simple and demanding: 'Come to me' (Matthew 11:28). It is remarkable how reluctant we often are, faced with a worry, anxiety, problem or difficulty, to respond to such a simple invitation. Something in human nature obstinately insists that we can cope on our own. Children may run to their parents when they need help, but as adults we often prefer to fight it out in our own strength.

It requires true humility, which is an essential element of faith, to bow our heads and accept both the yoke and the gracious strength of our divine partner.

Reflection

'Come to me' is such a simple invitation. Why does it sometimes seem so difficult to do?

DAVID WINTER

The resurrection and the life

Martha said to Jesus, 'Lord, if you had been here, my brother would not have died. But even now I know that God will give you whatever you ask of him.' Jesus said to her, 'Your brother will rise again.' Martha said to him, 'I know that he will rise again in the resurrection on the last day.' Jesus said to her, 'I am the resurrection and the life. Those who believe in me, even though they die, will live, and everyone who lives and believes in me will never die. Do you believe this?' She said to him, 'Yes, Lord, I believe that you are the Messiah, the Son of God, the one coming into the world.'

Lazarus, whom Jesus 'loved', had died and now, after a mysterious delay, Jesus is visiting his grieving sisters at the family home in Bethany. Both Mary and Martha greet him with what seems to be a rebuke: 'If you had been here, my brother would not have died.' It is as though the grieving mind needs to find someone to blame.

Jesus deflects this comment with a simple statement of faith: 'Your brother will rise again' (v. 23). Do I detect in Martha's response a slightly dismissive tone when she says, 'I know that he will rise again in the resurrection on the last day' (v. 24)? The implication seems to be, 'That may be right and true, but we miss him now.' To that Jesus responds with one of his greatest affirmations: 'I am the resurrection and the life' (v. 25). What did he mean?

The prologue to this Gospel claims that in Jesus, the Word, was 'life' (1:3). He is 'resurrection' (11:25) because in him the very life of the Creator dwells. Consequently, as he now elaborates to Mary, 'those who believe in me' (v. 25) also share in that life. They have already, right now, 'passed from death to life' (5:24). Jesus then challenges Martha, 'Do you believe this?' (v. 26). In reply, she wisely avoids the word 'this' (that is, his mind-blowing claim) and simply says, 'Yes, Lord, I believe you are the Messiah' (v. 27). That is it, really!

Reflection

In the end, it is not what we believe, but who we believe in that matters.

DAVID WINTER

Supper at Emmaus

As they came near the village to which they were going, he walked ahead as if he were going on. But they urged him strongly, saying, 'Stay with us, because it is almost evening and the day is now nearly over.' So he went in to stay with them. When he was at the table with them, he took bread, blessed and broke it, and gave it to them. Then their eyes were opened, and they recognised him; and he vanished from their sight. They said to each other, 'Were not our hearts burning within us while he was talking to us on the road, while he was opening the scriptures to us?'

Presumably this couple, walking disconsolately home to Emmaus from Jerusalem on the Sunday after the crucifixion, are Mr and Mrs Clopas (or Cleopas—see John 19:25). Disciples of Jesus, they are, understandably, at a low ebb. As they explain to the stranger who has joined them on their journey, 'We had hoped that he [Jesus] was the one to redeem Israel' (24:21). The stranger then starts a long exposition of the scriptures relating to the Messiah and what would happen to him.

Our passage begins when they reach their house. As it is almost evening, they persuade the stranger to stay with them. A meal is prepared and the visitor is invited to give thanks. He takes the bread, blesses and breaks it and gives it to them. Perhaps a year or so earlier they had been present when Jesus did exactly that in front of 5000 people. At any rate, in that moment 'their eyes were opened, and they recognised him' (v. 31). It was Jesus himself. Though he then withdrew from their sight, they could not wait to go and share this news with the others. The seven long miles back to Jerusalem seemed nothing to their speeding feet! His Bible study had stirred their hearts, but, as they explained, 'he had been made known to them in the breaking of the bread' (v. 35). So, in one lovely story, Luke encapsulates the two most powerful ways of encountering the Lord Jesus: scripture and sacrament.

Reflection

The risen Jesus met the disciples in their disappointment. He still does.

David Winter

How to do everything

Above all, clothe yourselves with love, which binds everything together in perfect harmony. And let the peace of Christ rule in your hearts, to which indeed you were called in the one body. And be thankful. Let the word of Christ dwell in you richly; teach and admonish one another in all wisdom; and with gratitude in your hearts sing psalms, hymns, and spiritual songs to God. And whatever you do, in word or deed, do everything in the name of the Lord Jesus, giving thanks to God the Father through him.

Sundays were very long for Christians in first-century Colosse. Early in the morning they gathered across the city for the 'breaking of bread'. This would have been a solemn but joyous occasion, led by the local presbyters and deacons, with scripture read and preached, prayer and worship shared and the sacred ordinance celebrated. They would then go off to work, Sundays being working days in the Roman Empire.

In the evening, however, it seems that they gathered again, but then in what the writer to the Hebrews calls episynagogues—literally, extra meetings (10:25). This passage offers the modern reader a fascinating glimpse into what a 'home meeting' was like in the first century. They prayed, studied the scriptures (especially the teaching of Jesus, the 'word of Christ') and challenged and encouraged each other. They also sang—'psalms and hymns and spiritual songs'. That was quite a musical mix, from the chanting of the Hebrew psalms to the hymns of the early church and something probably like our worship songs.

In a final word of advice to these groups, Paul gives them an all-encompassing touchstone for their lives. Whatever they do—in their meetings, at home, at work or in the marketplace—they are to do it gratefully and 'in the name of the Lord Jesus'.

Reflection

Can I do it 'in the name of the Lord Jesus' (Colossians 3:17)? If I can't, should I be doing it at all?

DAVID WINTER

All made new!

Then I saw a new heaven and a new earth; for the first heaven and the first earth had passed away, and the sea was no more. And I saw the holy city, the new Jerusalem, coming down out of heaven from God, prepared as a bride adorned for her husband. And I heard a loud voice from the throne saying, 'See, the home of God is among mortals. He will dwell with them as their God; they will be his peoples, and God himself will be with them; he will wipe every tear from their eyes. Death will be no more; mourning and crying and pain will be no more, for the first things have passed away.' And the one who was seated on the throne said, 'See, I am making all things new.'

This is where it will all end—in the 'new' Jerusalem, the kingdom of heaven itself. The Bible's richest image is found here in its last few pages, in the book of Revelation.

In the 'old' Jerusalem, there was a temple and, within the temple, there was the holy place where the Jewish people could recognise the presence of God among them. Of course, as we saw in King Solomon's words (1 Kings 8:27–30, 2 May), God doesn't literally dwell in human buildings, however lofty, beautiful and sacred they are. One day, though, we are promised, there will be a 'new' Jerusalem. It will not need a temple to represent God's presence among his people because, actually, permanently and gloriously, he will dwell among them—literally, 'make his home'. He will dry our tears and put an end to mourning, pain and death. Everything will be made 'new'.

In his Son, Jesus, God came to where we were and, in the language of John's Gospel, 'tabernacled' ('pitched his tent') for a while among us (1:14), literally. Today's Bible passage shows us that God himself—Father, Son and Holy Spirit—will one day be among his people forever.

Reflection

The new Jerusalem, the kingdom of heaven, is a community of love, truth and beauty, with God himself at its very heart. This is the future!

DAVID WINTER

17

After Pentecost: Acts 27—28

The last two chapters of Acts contain a whole lot of drama, mostly centred on sailing. My own experience of sailing is limited and embarrassing—I flunked my capsize drill and managed to crash a 1930s Broads boat that had been used in the television dramatisation of Arthur Ransome's *Swallows and Amazons*!

For Paul and his companions, however, the sea was the superhighway of the Middle East—far quicker than land travel, if somewhat more hazardous. We know from Romans 1:15 that Paul was eager to visit the new church in Rome, to which he had so far only written a letter, and to use his gifts to win more people to join it. Perhaps he had not planned to go there as a prisoner, but, as he was a Roman citizen by birth (Acts 22:25–29), he had the right to appeal to the Emperor. As well as wanting to seek justice, it must also have occurred to him that this was an unexpected opportunity to go and bring the good news to the heart of the Empire.

The use of 'we' in these chapters indicates that Luke, the author of Acts, travelled with him—whether as a friend, a colleague, a doctor or to record the journey, we do not know. Nor do we know at what point Luke left Paul in Rome. What we do know is that Paul's faith and determination held firm through many difficulties and dangers, some of them life-threatening, and he got to where he wanted to be (and managed to get all his fellow travellers, including his jailer, safely to Rome as well).

Most of us will reach a point in life (usually after 40, but it can come earlier) when we wonder what happened to the dreams and goals we started with and if we have taken entirely the wrong path in our career or relationships. Yesterday, on Facebook, I saw this post: 'God will always provide. It just might look different from what we had in mind.' I believe that God has our destination prepared, but the route taken might not be what we envisaged at all. Paul's route was indirect, bumpy and tiring, but he arrived in one piece.

Veronica Zundel

The slow lane

When it was decided that we were to sail for Italy, they transferred Paul and some other prisoners to a centurion of the Augustan Cohort, named Julius. Embarking on a ship of Adramyttium... we put to sea... The next day we put in at Sidon; and Julius treated Paul kindly, and allowed him to go to his friends to be cared for. Putting out to sea from there, we sailed under the lee of Cyprus, because the winds were against us. After we had sailed across the sea that is off Cilicia and Pamphylia, we came to Myra in Lycia. There the centurion found an Alexandrian ship bound for Italy and put us on board. We sailed slowly for a number of days and arrived with difficulty off Cnidus, and as the wind was against us, we sailed under the lee of Crete off Salmone. Sailing past it with difficulty, we came to a place called Fair Havens, near the city of Lasea.

I have just booked our summer holiday online. Unfortunately, I got one digit wrong in the payment card's expiry date and, for correcting this, the company charged us £27, making our flight the most expensive of the three I looked at instead of the cheapest!

The perils of booking online are nothing to what Paul and his companions faced on their journey to Rome. For a start, they were going the long way, stopping at every port along the coast. Second, their ship only went as far as Myra, where they had to change. Most significantly, the winds were against them, so they progressed 'with difficulty'. All because Paul decided he wanted to go to the top of the Roman hierarchy to seek justice.

What a relief it must have been for Paul to stay with his friends in Sidon, then later to arrive at the promisingly named Fair Havens. There were many more hazards to come, however.

Recently I saw a news report of a nun arrested for protesting at a nuclear site. Like Paul, she took a risk because of her commitment to God's kingdom. I do not know if I would be as brave.

Prayer

Lord, whatever dangers face me in serving you, be there when I meet them.

VERONICA ZUNDEL

The shipping news

Since much time had been lost and sailing was now dangerous, because even the Fast had already gone by, Paul advised them, saying, 'Sirs, I can see that the voyage will be with danger and much heavy loss, not only of the cargo and the ship, but also of our lives.' But the centurion paid more attention to the pilot and to the owner of the ship than to what Paul said. Since the harbour was not suitable for spending the winter, the majority was in favour of putting to sea from there, on the chance that somehow they could reach Phoenix, where they could spend the winter.

There is something very comforting about the 'liturgy' of the shipping forecast on Radio 4. Carol Ann Duffy, Poet Laureate, uses its rhythmical sound in a well-known sonnet about 'the radio's prayer': Rockall; Malin; Dogger; Finisterre. For those actually at sea, knowing the forecast may be a matter of life and death. Sailors know, as those carrying Paul did, that it can be much riskier to travel in winter weather than at other times of the year. The Day of Atonement, always in the autumn, had passed and soon it would be unsafe in the relatively small sailing boats of the day. Better to stay in harbour till spring came.

Paul, in no hurry to reach his trial in Rome, reminds the captain and crew of this. Perhaps he also has some insight from God about the progress of the journey. Julius the centurion, though impressed with Paul, as we saw yesterday, evidently had more confidence in the experienced hands on board. Besides, they might reach a better harbour.

Ships are not designed for staying in the harbour, as preachers like to tell us. Nor are Christians designed for staying in safe places enjoying the presence of God. There are times, though, when the harbour is where God wants us to be, to prepare us for further travelling or to let us recover from our last journey. There are also times when we are called to set out into the storms in faith. We need discernment to tell which is which.

Reflection

'For everything there is a season, and a time for every matter under heaven' (Ecclesiastes 3:1).

VERONICA ZUNDEL

ACTS 27:13–20 (NRSV, ABRIDGED)

In peril on the sea

When a moderate south wind began to blow, they thought they could achieve their purpose; so they weighed anchor and began to sail past Crete, close to the shore. But soon a violent wind, called the northeaster, rushed down from Crete. Since the ship was caught and could not be turned head-on into the wind, we gave way to it and were driven... Then, fearing that they would run on the Syrtis, they lowered the sea anchor... We were being pounded by the storm so violently that on the next day they began to throw the cargo overboard, and on the third day... they threw the ship's tackle overboard. When neither sun nor stars appeared for many days, and no small tempest raged, all hope of our being saved was at last abandoned.

For modern people, a rough sea journey usually means no more than sea sickness. For a first-century sailing vessel, it was a different story. The sailors now believed Paul's prediction of 'much heavy loss' (Acts 27:10). Paul himself and his companion Luke were probably reconciled to their own imminent death—after all, Paul had written, 'my desire is to depart and be with Christ, for that is far better' (Philippians 1:23).

It is ironic that Luke writes, 'All hope of our being saved was at last abandoned' (Acts 27:20), since he knew that, in the wider sense, he and Paul were already saved. This does not mean that they were not afraid: both must have wanted to live and continue their ministries of preaching and writing. If they had not survived this trip, we would never have had the book of Acts.

Clearly it is not wrong to want to continue on this earth as long as we can, to 'work the works of him who sent me while it is day', as Jesus said (John 9:4). When we are caught in a literal or metaphorical storm, we may sometimes wish we could die and meet God, but God may have prepared more good works for us to do right here.

Prayer

'Oh, hear us when we cry to thee, for those in peril on the sea!' (William Whiting, 1860)—whether that peril is physical, emotional or spiritual.

VERONICA ZUNDEL

I told you so

Since they had been without food for a long time, Paul then stood up among them and said, 'Men, you should have listened to me and not have set sail from Crete and thereby avoided this damage and loss. I urge you now to keep up your courage, for there will be no loss of life among you, but only of the ship. For last night there stood by me an angel of the God to whom I belong and whom I worship, and he said, 'Do not be afraid, Paul; you must stand before the emperor; and indeed, God has granted safety to all those who are sailing with you.' So keep up your courage, men, for I have faith in God that it will be exactly as I have been told. But we will have to run aground on some island.'

Don't you just hate it when someone says, 'I told you it wouldn't work'? Paul's 'You should have listened to me' must, similarly, have been quite irritating for the captain and his crew. His message from God was probably more welcome.

Few on the ship would have been Christian, though some might have been convinced by Paul's message and his trust in God. This story tells us that God's blessings are not confined to those who believe—indeed, sometimes it may seem that unbelievers are more blessed than believers (Psalm 73:2–5). We should never simply judge anybody as a wicked person who will eventually pay for their sins, however (Psalm 73:16–18). God might just be protecting them until they can encounter Jesus for themselves.

Now the ship's pilot and sailors have to make a hard decision. They have already lost their cargo and tackle and now Paul is urging them to run aground deliberately, losing their ship, too. To save our lives, we may have to let go of things we value greatly, even our very livelihood. It is not an easy choice and, in order to make it, we need to have a strong concept of God's goodness.

Reflection

'For those who want to save their life will lose it, and those who lose their life for my sake will save it' (Luke 9:24).

VERONICA ZUNDEL

ACTS 27:27–32 (NRSV, ABRIDGED)

On and on

When the fourteenth night had come, as we were drifting across the sea of Adria, about midnight the sailors suspected that they were nearing land... Fearing that we might run on the rocks, they let down four anchors from the stern and prayed for day to come. But when the sailors tried to escape from the ship and had lowered the boat into the sea, on the pretext of putting out anchors from the bow, Paul said to the centurion and the soldiers, 'Unless these men stay in the ship, you cannot be saved.' Then the soldiers cut away the ropes of the boat and set it adrift.

'How long, O Lord? Will you forget me for ever? How long will you hide your face from me? How long must I bear pain in my soul, and have sorrow in my heart all day long?' (Psalm 13:1–2). Paul and his companions may have prayed this psalm as the storm continued for a whole two weeks.

For many of us, our 'storm'—illness, work problems, unemployment, a disabled child, dependent parents, unwilling singleness, an unhappy marriage—may last for years with no suggestion that it will ever end. Having suffered fertility problems myself, I have a lot of sympathy with those who wait long years for a child. Some never have the longed-for baby, or their prayers are answered in some other way, such as adoption or an unexpected ministry. What happens to our faith when God never seems to answer these questions? It is tempting, if God doesn't appear to answer our prayers, to abandon our faith or 'make our own arrangements', manipulating events to get what we want.

Some of the sailors on Paul's ship, spying land approaching, seem to want to make their own arrangements, lowering the lifeboat ready to escape. If they had succeeded, Paul, Julius and his cohort would have been stranded, with no one to sail the ship. Paul, ever alert, intervenes: now they have no boat to get to shore, but at least the passengers have not been betrayed.

Reflection

'Trust God from the bottom of your heart; don't try to figure out everything on your own' (Proverbs 3:5, THE MESSAGE).

VERONICA ZUNDEL

Taste and see

Just before daybreak, Paul urged all of them to take some food, saying, 'Today is the fourteenth day that you have been in suspense and remaining without food, having eaten nothing. Therefore I urge you to take some food, for it will help you survive; for none of you will lose a hair from your heads.' After he had said this, he took bread; and giving thanks to God in the presence of all, he broke it and began to eat. Then all of them were encouraged and took food for themselves. (We were in all two hundred and seventy-six persons in the ship.) After they had satisfied their hunger, they lightened the ship by throwing the wheat into the sea.

If you have ever had sea sickness or an illness that made you lose your appetite, you will know what the people on this ship must have felt like. The last thing they wanted was food, yet it was the first thing they needed to build their strength up. Paul was a tentmaker as well as a rabbi, a practical man who could perhaps turn his hand to most things.

His gesture of breaking the bread, thanking God and sharing it reminds us of the risen Jesus' hosts at Emmaus, recognising him as he breaks bread, or of Jesus giving new significance to eating together at the last supper. Notice that Paul eats first himself, to encourage the others to eat something. The best spiritual leaders do not ask us to go through anything they have not experienced themselves—as Jesus demonstrated, taking up his own cross to show us how to take up ours (Mark 8:34).

Food must have become scarce by this point, as they had not touched land for two weeks. The bread Paul shared may even have been made from some of the grain the ship was carrying to sell. Now they have to throw the rest overboard to reach land. They are left with nothing but their lives. In the end, whatever assets we own, that is all we have to offer to God.

Prayer

'I have no silver or gold, but what I have I give you' (Acts 3:6). Make this your prayer of commitment to God.

VERONICA ZUNDEL

Safe on the shore

In the morning they did not recognise the land, but they noticed a bay with a beach, on which they planned to run the ship ashore... So they cast off the anchors and left them in the sea... then hoisting the foresail to the wind, they made for the beach. But striking a reef, they ran the ship aground... The soldiers' plan was to kill the prisoners, so that none might swim away and escape; but the centurion, wishing to save Paul, kept them from carrying out their plan. He ordered those who could swim to jump overboard first and make for the land, and the rest to follow, some on planks and others on pieces of the ship. And so it was that all were brought safely to land.

'I counted them all out... and I counted them all back,' said a TV newsman famously of a group of fighter jets in the 1982 Falklands conflict. Whatever we think about that or any war, I can understand why it is satisfying to say that of your own 'side' (if only we could say it of 'the other side' too).

The more I read of Julius the centurion, the more respect I have for him. No doubt afraid of punishment if they lost any prisoners, his men were all for killing them—sentencing them to death before they could even be tried—but Julius, having developed a liking for Paul (or even having become a Christian on the journey?) saves all to save one. This is the first we have heard of other prisoners on the ship and we do not know their crimes, but this just centurion will risk their escape to save what he clearly regards as an innocent man.

Children are always ready to say, 'It's not fair.' Does Jesus call us to be like children, because of that sense of fairness and unfairness (Matthew 18:3)? God, we are told, does not want any to perish (2 Peter 3:9). This will motivate some to evangelism, but others to bring food, shelter and education to the most vulnerable in the world. Both are equally valid callings.

Reflection

'Then they were glad because they had quiet, and he brought them to their desired haven' (Psalm 107:30)

VERONICA ZUNDEL

Saint or sinner?

After we had reached safety, we then learned that the island was called Malta. The natives showed us unusual kindness. Since it had begun to rain and was cold, they kindled a fire and welcomed all of us around it. Paul had gathered a bundle of brushwood and was putting it on the fire, when a viper, driven out by the heat, fastened itself on his hand. When the natives saw the creature hanging from his hand, they said to one another, 'This man must be a murderer; though he has escaped from the sea, justice has not allowed him to live.' He, however, shook off the creature into the fire and suffered no harm... After they had waited a long time and saw that nothing unusual had happened to him, they changed their minds and began to say that he was a god.

Whenever any disaster happens, some Christians rush to suggest that it is God's punishment on whatever group of people or social trend they disapprove of. Personally, I do not believe the Father of Jesus is a punishing God. Even in the Old Testament, the overwhelming theme is God's mercy, forgiveness and patience.

Of course, that sort of punishment theory is not confined to Christians. The people of Malta here are convinced that if you get bitten by a snake, you must have done something badly wrong. They had not heard the word 'karma', but they would understand the concept. A few hours later, though, when Paul has not dropped dead, they do an about turn and declare that he is a god (not the first time he has been deified—see Acts 14:11–12). There is nothing so fickle as public opinion, as Jesus found in Holy Week.

We humans like extremes, painting people as either heroes or monsters. In reality, the line between good and evil runs right through the centre of the human heart. We are all born capable of great good or terrible evil. Paul was no different—he had, after all, been a torturer. God works with the flawed but unique material that is to hand.

Reflection

'Jesus answered, "Neither this man nor his parents sinned; he was born blind so that God's works might be revealed in him"' (John 9:2).

VERONICA ZUNDEL

ACTS 28:7–10 (NRSV)

One good turn

Now in the neighbourhood of that place were lands belonging to the leading man of the island, named Publius, who received us and entertained us hospitably for three days. It so happened that the father of Publius lay sick in bed with fever and dysentery. Paul visited him and cured him by praying and putting his hands on him. After this happened, the rest of the people on the island who had diseases also came and were cured. They bestowed many honours on us, and when we were about to sail, they put on board all the provisions we needed.

How lovely it is when, after great difficulty or distress, we come to a time of recovery and blessing. This is expressed beautifully in George Herbert's poem 'The Flower' (*The Temple*, 1633): 'How fresh, O Lord, how sweet and clean/Are thy returns! ev'n as the flowers in spring.'

Like the centurion Julius, the governor Publius is a caring and generous man. He feeds and shelters the prisoners without hope of reward. Would you or I so quickly take in some stray travellers charged with offences against the State? Clearly, Paul had the gift of making friends wherever he went. Perhaps it was the result of his resolve to be 'all things to all people' (1 Corinthians 9:22). We need not be like the hero of Woody Allen's film *Zelig*, a man who took on the traits of whoever he was with, in order to be flexible and adapt ourselves to the people we find ourselves meeting.

Publius, in fact, does get a reward: the healing of his father, which leads to the healing of many others. He would have made a good witness at Paul's trial in Rome. He evidently 'knew Paul by his fruits', even if he did not espouse Paul's 'strange' new teaching.

Can we recognise the good in others, even when we do not necessarily agree with their beliefs or lifestyle? I believe that God's image in all humans is not erased by sin, only (sometimes heavily) disguised. If we call out the good in others, we will help them to recognise Jesus—so long as they also see his goodness in us.

Prayer

Lord Jesus, teach me to see 'that of God' in every human being.

VERONICA ZUNDEL

Retreating to advance

Three months later we set sail on a ship that had wintered at the island, an Alexandrian ship with the Twin Brothers as its figure-head. We put in at Syracuse and stayed there for three days; then we weighed anchor and came to Rhegium. After one day there a south wind sprang up, and on the second day we came to Puteoli. There we found believers and were invited to stay with them for seven days. And so we came to Rome. The believers from there, when they heard of us, came as far as the Forum of Appius and Three Taverns to meet us. On seeing them, Paul thanked God and took courage. When we came into Rome, Paul was allowed to live by himself, with the soldier who was guarding him.

They say, if you fall off your bicycle, the best thing is to get straight back on. Paul and the other prisoners, however, probably were not that keen to set foot on a ship again. So, perhaps it was a blessing that they had to stay in Malta until the winter ended. Malta still has a Christian history of which it is proud—clearly Paul and Luke did not waste their time there.

Sometimes we are stuck, maybe for years, in a situation that we have not chosen and find hard to accept—caring for a parent with dementia, for instance. We may have ambitions that we have to put off, dreams we fear we will never fulfil. Can we see these times as an opportunity to do or learn something else we had not planned? Can we find places to rest and people to support us as Paul did at Puteoli?

All bad (or mixed) things come to an end. 'And so we came to Rome' (v. 14)—the place where Paul most wanted to proclaim the good news. Of course, he was not the first Christian to do so; there was already a church there, to whom he had written his most famous letter. He seems to have accepted that his role was not to found the church in Rome, but be supported by it. Can we accept receiving when we wanted to give?

Reflection
'I planted, Apollos watered, but God gave the growth'
(1 Corinthians 3:6).

VERONICA ZUNDEL

His own people

Three days later [Paul] called together the local leaders of the Jews... He said to them, 'Brothers, though I had done nothing against our people or the customs of our ancestors, yet I was arrested in Jerusalem and handed over to the Romans. When they had examined me, the Romans wanted to release me, because there was no reason for the death penalty in my case. But when the Jews objected, I was compelled to appeal to the emperor... For this reason therefore I have asked to see you and speak with you, since it is for the sake of the hope of Israel that I am bound with this chain.' They replied, 'We have received no letters from Judea about you, and none of the brothers coming here has reported or spoken anything evil about you. But we would like to hear from you what you think, for with regard to this sect we know that everywhere it is spoken against.'

Do you find that it is your own non-Christian family and closest friends to whom it is hardest to talk about your faith? They know all your faults and you cannot pretend with them. They may also be worried by your faith, wondering if you have lost the plot or joined an abusive cult.

Paul knows his call is to the Gentiles, yet he makes one more attempt to reach his fellow Jews. He cannot bear for them not to see Jesus. Perhaps, being human, he also wants to make his innocence clear in front of the Jews in Rome, who may be readier to accept his message than those in Jerusalem. Indeed they are, as, cut off from gossip about him, they are prepared to take him at face value and hear what he has to say—even though everything they have heard about the 'Jesus sect' is negative. They, like the Beroeans (Acts 17:11), set aside their prejudice and consider the evidence.

Romans 9—11 demonstrates how important the Jewish people still are in Paul's theology. My summary of these chapters goes, 'You do not have to be Jewish to be a Christian, but it helps.'

Prayer

Pray for one or two people you know well, whom you would like to know Jesus.

VERONICA ZUNDEL

Start where they are

> After they had set a day to meet with [Paul], they came to him at his lodgings in great numbers. From morning until evening he explained the matter to them, testifying to the kingdom of God and trying to convince them about Jesus both from the law of Moses and from the prophets. Some were convinced by what he had said, while others refused to believe.

This, like Jesus' walk to Emmaus, is one of those conversations on which one would so love to eavesdrop (the long sermon in Acts 20:9, which sent Eutychus to sleep, is one I can happily miss!). It is a whole day seminar with the greatest Christian teacher ever—what's not to like?

What is most impressive is Paul's contextualisation of his message. With pagans in Athens (Acts 17:16), he started his communication with one of the shrines of their own polytheistic faith. With his own people, he starts with their own scriptures, which the 'new faith' has by no means abandoned. He tries to convince them 'from the law of Moses and from the prophets'. Essentially, that means the whole of the Jewish scriptures, our Old Testament.

I do not always find it easy to find Jesus in the Old Testament. Sure, there are the great messianic prophetic passages such as Isaiah 53 or Moses' prediction in Deuteronomy of a greater prophet to come, but what do we do with the genocides in Joshua or the passages about God's anger? In some stories, God's behaviour does not strike me as very Jesus-like (not that Jesus did not get angry—he just did not do a lot of smiting).

Yet, my Mennonite tradition strives to read the whole Bible in the light of Jesus' life, death and resurrection, not interpret any of it independently of that. The key verse for me in interpreting the Bible is Hebrews 1:1: 'Long ago God spoke to our ancestors in many and various ways by the prophets, but in these last days he has spoken to us by a Son.' The message of Jesus enables us to reread every part of the Bible through the lens of his non-violent, suffering love.

Reflection

'Whoever has seen me has seen the Father' (John 14:9).

VERONICA ZUNDEL

The crunch comes

So they disagreed with each other; and as they were leaving, Paul made one further statement: 'The Holy Spirit was right in saying to your ancestors through the prophet Isaiah, "Go to this people and say, 'You will indeed listen, but never understand, and you will indeed look, but never perceive. For this people's heart has grown dull, and their ears are hard of hearing, and they have shut their eyes; so that they might not look with their eyes, and listen with their ears, and understand with their heart and turn—and I would heal them.'" Let it be known to you then that this salvation of God has been sent to the Gentiles; they will listen.'

Last Sunday I preached about being assertive and some Bible characters whom I see as assertive. I had to explain that assertiveness is not being aggressive, nagging or getting your own way. It is about stating your case clearly and making sure you and the other person are both heard, whatever the outcome. I think Paul is being assertive here. Some Roman Jews have responded positively to his message; most have not. Some will join the Christian congregation who welcomed Paul to Rome or plant another one. Paul, however, sees that it is not worth saying any more to this group. He has done his best and, metaphorically, wipes the dust off his feet (Mark 6:11).

Some of you may have left a church because you no longer felt at home there, or your theology or theirs had changed, or you were unhappy with its leadership. Some are called to try to change things from the inside. Whichever group you belong to, there may come a time when you have to state your feelings clearly, as Paul does here.

It is hard to be a bearer of bad news. Paul had Luke and maybe other companions to support his stance. There is always value in testing your feelings or opinions with other people you trust. If the time for discussion is over, the Holy Spirit will tell us when it is time to give up and go.

Prayer
Lord, give wisdom to those who find themselves disagreeing with their closest friends.

VERONICA ZUNDEL

What happened to Paul?

[Paul] lived there two whole years at his own expense and welcomed all who came to him, proclaiming the kingdom of God and teaching about the Lord Jesus Christ with all boldness and without hindrance.

Facebook sometimes contains posts reminding people of a film or pop star of the past—perhaps followed by the question, 'Whatever happened to…?' Usually the answer is that they got older and less popular.

Similarly, we might ask, 'Whatever happened to Paul?' We leave him under house arrest, clearly earning a living, probably by tentmaking (perhaps friends brought him the materials and delivered the tents) or perhaps supported by the local church. After that, what? We simply do not know. We get the impression that Luke, the author of Acts, does not know either. This suggests the intriguing possibility that, at the time of writing, Paul's fate still was not determined. Was he tried and found guilty? Was he released? If that had been the case, surely we would know more about his later activities. Did he die of natural causes?

Perhaps it does not matter. We do know that he did not let his lack of mobility stop him sharing the good news. He kept an open house, witnessing to all who came. Ephesians 6:20 describes Paul as 'an ambassador in chains'—an evocative expression that puts me in mind of Nelson Mandela, in prison for 27 years, yet emerging ready to be his country's president, or Aung San Suu Kyi, under house arrest for a decade, yet still able to build an opposition party in Burma.

I wonder what 'chains' could prevent us from sharing Jesus with others. Shyness? Doubts? Fear that our lives do not match up to our message? Imagining we have to be as effective as Paul? Really, all we need to do is tell others, when the opportunity arises, what we have experienced of God, however little it seems. Paul's opportunities come from his exercising hospitality, which is something many of us can do. We do not have to be 'super-evangelists', chalking up souls on some divine scoreboard.

Prayer

Pray for opportunities to witness that are just right for you.

VERONICA ZUNDEL

Building God's kingdom on earth

'Once, on being asked by the Pharisees when the kingdom of God would come, Jesus replied, "The coming of the kingdom of God is not something that can be observed, nor will people say, 'Here it is,' or 'There it is,' because the kingdom of God is within you"' (Luke 17:21, NIV, with alternative wording).

When we imagine building God's kingdom, it is tempting to focus on externals—activities, organisations and personnel. Planting churches, establishing meetings or outreaches, training leaders, attracting followers, acquiring or renting buildings, producing literature, creating community links and networks, making our voices heard. As we do this, funds and attendance numbers are never far from our minds.

The kingdom of God, however, is a reign, not a territory; and the essence of building God's kingdom is the inner work of love and faith in the disciple's heart. Without that, results will be hollow even if they are grand. As we spend the next few days thinking about what it means to build the kingdom of God on earth, we will be focusing on the core qualities foundational to the outer work we build on them.

Of course, love that never makes it through to any kind of practical action exists primarily on the plane of the imagination. The Messiah who said, 'the Son of Man did not come to be served but to serve' (Mark 10:45), had it in mind that our conversion of heart would be expressed in how we involve ourselves with others. We run the risk of empire-building rather than bringing in the kingdom, however, if we do not first engage with the soul work that establishes our spiritual priorities and objectives.

As we reflect and pray, we align ourselves with God's will, to make ready for action. You might like to use the following prayer at the beginning of our studies:

God of all truth, your seed is sown in the human heart and your kingdom is not 'here' or 'there' but within me. As I study and pray, make me sensitive to your still small voice, your presence and transformative power, giving me the grace so to open my life to your Spirit that through me your sovereignty may be made visible; for I ask it in Jesus' name. Amen

Penelope Wilcock

Putting the Lord first

This is what the Lord Almighty says: 'Give careful thought to your ways. Go up into the mountains and bring down timber and build my house, so that I may take pleasure in it and be honoured,' says the Lord. 'You expected much, but see, it turned out to be little. What you brought home, I blew away. Why?' declares the Lord Almighty. 'Because of my house, which remains a ruin, while each of you is busy with your own house.'

The first and most obvious thing about a kingdom is that it has a monarch. It is a nation with a supreme ruler.

The root of the word 'nation' is to do with being born—native, née—it is the place I come from, my homeland, where I belong; the place that determines who I am. So the beginning of the kingdom is to do with spiritual birth—being 'born again' into a new heritage under the sovereignty of God. His reign determines my identity.

When we become the subjects of God's kingdom, we give up our will for his. The prospect of this might make us feel uneasy—as if we were to become puppets, with God pulling the strings—but that is not how it is. The will of God is reality, truth, love. In becoming his, what we give up is the posing and selfish ambitions of the ego; we lose nothing worth having, for we are born into abundant life.

Certainly the life of the kingdom is not without struggle: we can see its ultimate cost in the prayer of Jesus at Gethsemane—'Yet not as I will, but as you will' (Matthew 26:39). He gave his life, in obedience to his heavenly king. The blessings of the kingdom, however, are ours in lives transformed: 'if anyone is in Christ, the new creation has come: the old has gone, the new is here!' (2 Corinthians 5:17).

Watchpoint: We begin with a change of priorities—God is on the throne.

Prayer
Sovereign Lord, humbly I offer you my life. All I am and have is yours, for you are my king. Teach me and lead me in your ways, O God of glory.
Amen

PENELOPE WILCOCK

The poor and lowly

'When you reap the harvest of your land, do not reap to the very edges of your field or gather the gleanings of your harvest. Leave them for the poor and for the foreigner residing among you. I am the Lord your God.'... Do not take a pair of millstones—not even the upper one—as security for a debt, because that would be taking a person's livelihood as security.

The values of God's kingdom challenge the ways of the world head on—turn them upside down at times: '"For my thoughts are not your thoughts, neither are your ways my ways," declares the Lord' (Isaiah 55:8). In the kingdoms of the world, we are used to the poor being exploited and disregarded—disenfranchised. 'Money talks,' they say, and, 'He who pays the piper calls the tune.' The life of Jesus, however, like the proclamations of the prophets of old, dare us to venture beyond familiar social and political conventions, letting justice, compassion and love redefine our value system.

'You will always have the poor among you,' Jesus says (John 12:8), but, though we accept this reality and do not lose ourselves in utopian dreams, in the kingdom we add in support and rescue, compassion and respect, as he showed us to do. People can often find the resources to overcome the disadvantages of poverty, provided they are helped and their dignity is honoured and they are not reduced to despair. Empowering others includes celebrating their participation as confidence and self-esteem come from discovering we have, after all, a valued contribution to make. The humane provision of the Law, in our passages for today, tempers the wind to the shorn lamb; it is about giving people a chance to get on their feet.

Watchpoint: We learn reverence for the poor in God's upside-down kingdom.

Prayer

O God, your reign is made known in Jesus, a homeless baby in a manger in Bethlehem, a wandering preacher, crucified and rejected, laid in a borrowed grave. Help me by your grace to see life through your eyes, recognising Jesus in the poor and outcast adrift on the streets where I live.

PENELOPE WILCOCK

Fair dealing

Do not have two differing weights in your bag—one heavy, one light. Do not have two differing measures in your house—one large, one small. You must have accurate and honest weights and measures, so that you may live long in the land the Lord your God is giving you. For the Lord your God detests anyone who does these things, anyone who deals dishonestly.

'Honesty is the best policy' is a well-known saying, but we are going deeper than that here. In the kingdom of God, honesty and integrity are not policies designed to keep us out of trouble, make us look good and get us our own way. They are not a marketing tool or promotional strategy to be dropped when no one is looking, but are to be the warp and weft of our thinking, our motivation, our expectation. Justice (with compassion) is a central kingdom value.

This extends beyond simply not cheating, to ensuring that right is part of every detail of our professional and household choices. Informing ourselves about our purchases—how their production systems affect the earth and the human community—is all part of building God's kingdom on earth. Tracing the components of every commodity we buy for their ethical and ecological track records is impossible, but we can be sure that making the decision to buy from small, local firms or farmers' markets, buying second-hand where possible, buying organically grown and compassionately farmed produce and choosing Fairtrade are part of what it means to take our Christian faith seriously.

We live a long way from the simple lifestyles of those among whom Jesus lived and taught, but we still bear the responsibility to love our neighbour. This, making choices shaped by an informed conscience, is part of the way we bring our daily life under the reign of God.

Watchpoint: Whatever we spend our money on, we bless and help prosper.

Prayer

Father, help me to make space each day to live responsibly as part of the worldwide human family. Open my eyes to see the potential of trade to be an opportunity to promote justice and an expression of allegiance to you.

PENELOPE WILCOCK

MATTHEW 7:15–18 (NIV)

Truth

[Jesus said] 'Watch out for false prophets. They come to you in sheep's clothing, but inwardly they are ferocious wolves. By their fruit you will recognise them. Do people pick grapes from thorn-bushes, or figs from thistles? Likewise, every good tree bears good fruit, but a bad tree bears bad fruit. A good tree cannot bear bad fruit, and a bad tree cannot bear good fruit.'

When we picture kings and queens, pageantry and splendour come to mind—soldiers uniformed in scarlet, a golden coach, sumptuous banquets—but the majesty of the kingdom of God does not reside in any kind of pomp. It is not that God dislikes colour and magnificence—he created sunsets and parrots, after all—but, as Irenaeus said in the second century, 'The glory of God is a human being fully alive.'

The authority and nobility of the kingdom are not an effect. They proceed not from display but from the quality of truth. This is expressed in honesty and unpretentiousness, in wisdom and insight. It is transformative—as Jesus said, 'the truth will set you free' (John 8:32). Both in the reality of personal authenticity and the revelation of divine love, truth is central to the building of God's kingdom on earth.

Of course, the perennial problem is how to discern the truth when we encounter it, especially when it meets us in unexpected people who do not resemble the authority figures of the culture we trust. How are we to differentiate the real thing from something that merely looks and sounds like it? In our reading today, Jesus tells us to look at how people live, their habits and actions—the fruit of the tree. He tells us this cannot lie. People who are kind, patient, loving, peaceable, responsible and gentle are the ones whose version of truth is to be trusted.

Watchpoint: 'Sanctify them through thy truth: thy word is truth' (John 17:17, KJV).

Prayer

God of truth, help me to be a straightforward, unaffected person, dependably honest, trusting in you, free of all prevarication and pretending, a plain believer and trustworthy servant of you. May I serve you in word and in action.

PENELOPE WILCOCK

Ascension Day

'Here I am! I stand at the door and knock. If anyone hears my voice and opens the door, I will come in and eat with that person, and they with me. To the one who is victorious, I will give the right to sit with me on my throne, just as I was victorious and sat down with my Father on his throne. Whoever has ears, let them hear what the Spirit says to the churches.'

When monarchs come into power, we say they 'ascend to the throne'. The ascension of Jesus, though it appears to be a departure, is a necessary stage, bringing him into a direct, dynamic relationship of authority with us, his subjects. In ascending to heaven, Jesus is not leaving us, but taking humanity into the Father's presence, opening the channel for the Holy Spirit at Pentecost. It is part of the sequence of events—his participation in creation, his coming as Emmanuel, his life and teaching, his passion, death and resurrection, his ascension, his outpouring of the Holy Spirit—that will culminate in his coming in glory.

In today's passage, Jesus says, 'Here I am!' That means two things: he is united with God (in the Bible, 'I Am' often means the Name of God) and he is directly and immediately present with us. As George Fox, founder of the Quakers, taught, 'Christ has come to teach his people himself.' We have no need for intermediaries, for he is with us in the inward light of his Holy Spirit.

Today's passage also speaks of Jesus sitting with the Father on the Father's throne, not Jesus having his own throne in heaven. There is no separation—he and the Father are one. So, as we become one with him, in obedience and faith as his subjects, so we, too, are drawn into unity with God, forming the kingdom of heaven.

Watchpoint: Today we celebrate Jesus enthroned in heaven and in our hearts.

Prayer

Thank you Father, that, in the ascension of Jesus, you established a live power connection, a sovereign order of authority, linking heaven and earth. May I discover freedom and confidence as I place my trust in Jesus, the Lord of my heart.

PENELOPE WILCOCK

Simplicity

Jesus looked at [the man] and loved him. 'One thing you lack,' he said. 'Go, sell everything you have and give to the poor, and you will have treasure in heaven. Then come, follow me.' At this the man's face fell. He went away sad, because he had great wealth. Jesus looked round and said to his disciples, 'How hard it is for the rich to enter the kingdom of God!'

Jesus insisted on simplicity in his followers. He went so far as to say, 'those of you who do not give up everything you have cannot be my disciples' (Luke 14:33). This seems a hard teaching indeed, until we realise what an insulating barrier is formed between us and God by anything we believe we 'own' or 'have'.

To understand, it helps to think about the name of God—'I AM WHO I AM'. We are made in God's image—lots of little 'I AMs'—and we become free, effective, alive, to the extent that we learn to reside in this inner nature, our connection with him.

The temptation is always to seek identity elsewhere—in belongings, status or occupation. Just as soon as I believe I am anything beyond the simple 'I am', defining myself by achievement or acquisition—'I am rich', 'I am clever', 'I am a graduate'—or even by what I perceive as failure—'I am poor', 'I am a loser', 'I am no good'—I start to lose my precious identity as a simple child of God. 'I am' is all I need.

That is why it is so hard for the wealthy to enter the kingdom of God—it is really difficult to maintain the original simplicity of the I AM if my life is burdened with responsibility and cluttered with possessions. They are like the brambles choking the growing seed of the word in the parable of the sower (Matthew 13:7).

Watchpoint: Simplicity is the freedom of the kingdom, our 'I AM' identity.

Prayer

Help me to walk as Jesus did, in the freedom of being the Son of God. Help me to choose simplicity, to trust in you alone, for your goodness and mercy will uphold me every day of my life.

Penelope Wilcock

Inclusivity

Then Jesus' mother and brothers arrived. Standing outside, they
sent someone in to call him. A crowd was sitting round him, and
they told him, 'Your mother and brothers are outside looking for
you.' 'Who are my mother and my brothers?' he asked. Then he
looked at those seated in a circle round him and said, 'Here are
my mother and my brothers! Whoever does God's will is my
brother and sister and mother.'

Jesus made startling and radical modifications to the cultural norms
into which he was born. The changes he instigated were all about kindness and inclusivity—talking to a Samaritan woman, healing the daughter of a Gentile, allowing Mary of Bethany to sit with the men as a
disciple and, in today's passage, redefining 'tribe' and 'clan' to be acces-
sible by choice and belief rather than the closed destiny of birth or
limited by marriage.

When he called Matthew the tax-gatherer and Simon the Zealot to rub
along together in his group of disciples—and entrusted their common
purse to Judas the thief—Jesus taught his friends what inclusivity meant.
When he healed the Gerasene demoniac and restored him to his community and called the outcast Zacchaeus down from his tree to share his
supper, Jesus was letting his life teach about inclusivity. When he welcomed the noisy, sticky little children that his disciples had instinctively
shooed away, he left a lesson about inclusivity that we sometimes still
struggle to take in. Heaven is meant to be for everyone.

The church expresses the kingdom exactly to the extent of its inclusivity. The more rule-bound it is, the more deeply enmeshed in hierarchy and tradition, the harder it is to walk in the freedom of the good
news that offers each one of us a place in God's family, making us his
heirs by adoption through grace.

Watchpoint: A clique cannot coexist with the kingdom.

Prayer

*Thank you for the privilege of having Jesus as my brother. Help me to foster
the kindness of the kingdom in everyday life. Help me to maintain boundaries of dignity and respect but demolish walls of exclusion and division.*

PENELOPE WILCOCK

LUKE 17:1, 3–4 (NIV)

Forgiveness

Jesus said to his disciples: 'Things that cause people to stumble are bound to come, but woe to anyone through whom they come... So watch yourselves. If your brother or sister sins against you, rebuke them; and if they repent, forgive them. Even if they sin against you seven times in a day and seven times come back to you saying 'I repent,' you must forgive them.'

The kingdom of God cannot happen without forgiveness. Its coming is blocked wherever people refuse to forgive.

The kingdom is begun by God's willingness to forgive us unconditionally and continued as we, in turn, forgive. The citizens of God's kingdom live in the service of God, which is perfect freedom, and, like simplicity and truth, forgiveness sets us free. It uncouples us from dependency on the whim of others, so that their behaviour no longer determines who and what we become. Forgiveness breaks the links in chains that bind us. It sets those who have hurt us free to make a fresh start and allows us to walk away freely from painful events, not crippled by rancour or desire for vengeance. It is the material out of which new beginnings are made.

Forgiveness does not necessarily make us feel affectionate towards those who have hurt us. It may be appropriate to maintain boundaries that prevent unscrupulous or predatory or mentally ill people from having too free access to us. Forgiveness does not mean inviting trouble or encouraging others to take advantage of us. It is about releasing people from invisible debts—emotional, psychological, spiritual—and sometimes visible debts like money, too. Forgiveness is spiritual gardening, uprooting the invasive weeds of bitterness and resentment that would choke the sweeter blooms if left unchecked. It is hard work, but it makes our lives a more pleasant, healthier place to be.

Watchpoint: In forgiving others, I set myself free.

Prayer

God of mercy, thank you for the cross of Jesus that sets me free from sin, and your love that lets me start again. Wherever the sin of my brothers and sisters cuts into my life, may I, too, have the courage to choose forgiveness.

PENELOPE WILCOCK

Humility

Jesus called [the disciples] together and said, 'You know that the rulers of the Gentiles lord it over them, and their high officials exercise authority over them. Not so with you. Instead, whoever wants to become great among you must be your servant, and whoever wants to be first must be your slave—just as the Son of Man did not come to be served, but to serve, and to give his life as a ransom for many.'

Being humble is not the same as being a doormat. Jesus gave his life to the service of others—teaching, healing, washing their feet and, eventually, dying to create the bridge of love between heaven and earth—but nobody pushed him around. He made his choices freely, resisting every attempt to bully and coerce him. He spoke up fearlessly when necessary, having the courage for the ministry that Quakers call 'speaking truth to power'—challenging authority even when it is dangerous to do so.

His humility is not the false modesty of a person who pretends to be less than he is—there was nothing obsequious about Jesus! He would never curry favour with anyone and his speech was candid and direct. Nonetheless, he, King of heaven, was content with the hospitality of ordinary people; he was willing to do the work of a servant and lay down his life for his friends. His humility was the unquestioning acceptance of the perfect will of God.

Humility is the sweetness of the air in God's kingdom. Gently, unobtrusively, without arrogance or spite, his citizens go about their daily business. Quietly, without demanding or insisting, they get things done. There is no culture of blame in the kingdom of God; the citizens accept their responsibilities rather than insisting on their rights.

Watchpoint: In humble submission to God I find true confidence.

Prayer

God of miracles, wonder-worker, amaze me again—make me humble! Give me the grace to accept insignificance and lowliness, knowing that real stature and achievement lie in learning to love. Teach me the kindness I need to serve others willingly, the imagination to treat them with sensitivity and the gentleness that reveals the humility of the peaceable kingdom.

PENELOPE WILCOCK

MATTHEW 14:27–31 (NIV)

Failure

Jesus immediately said to them: 'Take courage! It is I. Don't be afraid.' 'Lord, if it's you,' Peter replied, 'tell me to come to you on the water.' 'Come,' he said. Then Peter got down out of the boat, walked on the water and came towards Jesus. But when he saw the wind, he was afraid and, beginning to sink, cried out, 'Lord, save me!' Immediately Jesus reached out his hand and caught him. 'You of little faith,' he said, 'why did you doubt?'

Being realistic, if we really intend to roll up our sleeves and get stuck into building God's kingdom on earth, we had better be prepared for some misfires and failures. Indeed it is impressive—shocking, even—how thick and fast our failures pile up as we make this great attempt of bringing the kingdom of heaven into the all too earthly context of our everyday lives.

Someone once rightly described 'failure' as not an incontrovertible fact but a point of view. Our failures are the waymarks of our willingness to try, our brave hope. Without failure, we can never learn wisdom or develop necessary life skills. Every failure is the sign of someone who was willing to have a go.

We might focus on Peter's humiliating loss of nerve and sinking under the waves, but we could choose, instead, to see the magnificence of his faith. Rather than see a man who nearly drowned, why not choose to recognise the one man in all history who walked with Jesus on water, who had the courage to get out of the boat.

Failure is inevitable for those who dream big, who take on the work of realising the vision of how beautiful life could be. If failure is certain, though, equally sure is the hand of Jesus, held out to pick us up and help us start again.

Watchpoint: Our failures are the many stepping stones on the way of grace.

Prayer

Loving Lord Jesus, better than anyone you know my failures. Please forgive the many times I have let you down and help me be as patient with the disappointments I encounter in others as you have been with my own.

PENELOPE WILCOCK

Peace

The wolf will live with the lamb, the leopard will lie down with the goat, the calf and the lion and the yearling together; and a little child will lead them... The infant will play near the cobra's den, the young child will put its hand into the viper's nest. They will neither harm nor destroy on all my holy mountain, for the earth will be filled with the knowledge of the Lord as the waters cover the sea.

Peace. We pray for it, we dream of it, we say it is what we long for. 'World peace', 'peace of mind', 'peace at last', 'peace and quiet'—these are apparently high on our agenda while also inexplicably scarce in our own experience. Perhaps, in part, this is because a prerequisite of peace is self-discipline. Family life will not be orderly and free from incessant bickering without self-discipline exercised and taught by parents. National and international life cannot be peaceful without giving as high a priority to others' interests as to one's own. Inner peace cannot be achieved without heeding and following the whisper of conscience.

Peace requires work, restraint and determination. Ease and complacency can look like peace, but they carry the seeds of war because they are self-indulgent.

In Isaiah's beautiful vision here of the holy mountain, the predator lays aside self-interest in astonishing restraint, while the preyed upon and vulnerable discover what it is to trust and live without fear. As they learn to live in mutual gentleness, they are led by innocence. This vision is meant as a parable, not a record of a freak of nature. It asks us to take up the challenge of learning gentleness, trust and restraint, so that communities of diversity may flourish in peace.

Those who would build the peaceable kingdom know to take a long view and remember that flesh and blood are never our enemy, only the forces of cruelty and oppression.

Watchword: Let there be peace on earth, dear Lord—and let it begin with me.

Prayer

Father, in you alone I find peace. Help me to choose your way. Nurture in me the heart of a peacemaker, as I work to build your kingdom.

PENELOPE WILCOCK

Equality

So in Christ Jesus you are all children of God through faith, for all of you who were baptised into Christ have clothed yourselves with Christ. There is neither Jew nor Gentile, neither slave nor free, nor is there male and female, for you are all one in Christ Jesus. If you belong to Christ, then you are Abraham's seed, and heirs according to the promise.

Sometimes it helps to look at where the Bible is going rather than where it is at, because its truth is more dynamic than static. It is not merely a rulebook for maintaining the status quo but also the inspiration for the unfolding gospel of our lives. As we read, we see the great heroes of the faith learning and changing, growing beyond their old preconceptions to new insights.

So it is here, with Paul encouraging slaves to obey their masters, yet elsewhere his wonderfully diplomatic letter to Philemon shows that he supports freedom from slavery. The apostles respected the customs of Jewish Law, but when they saw the Holy Spirit descend on the Gentiles, they realised that what God was doing took them beyond the Law's bounds. Paul's advice about women in church (silence, submission, covered heads) recommends that Christian people respect social custom and not bring their communities into disrepute, but the New Testament shows us glimpses of women in leadership.

The teaching and actions of Jesus stoutly defend the cause of women in society and children, too. On many occasions he pushed the boundaries of convention in favour of equality—in defending the woman taken in adultery, for example, and in rejecting the infamous 'divorce for any cause'. In the kingdom of heaven, all people are equal. Its citizens work towards a level playing field for everyone, but, on the way, we may have to learn to accept graciously that which is the best we can do for now.

Watchpoint: 'So in everything, do to others what you would have them do to you' (Matthew 7:12).

Prayer

Father, your love is for everyone—offered not as we deserve but as we need. Help me to love generously, believing and hoping the best for everyone.

PENELOPE WILCOCK

Reconciliation

You are no longer foreigners and strangers, but fellow citizens with God's people and also members of his household, built on the foundation of the apostles and prophets, with Christ Jesus himself as the chief cornerstone. In him the whole building is joined together and rises to become a holy temple in the Lord. And in him you too are being built together to become a dwelling in which God lives by his Spirit.

In the last prayer of Jesus (John 17), we see him pleading with the Father for unity among his followers—that we might be made as perfectly one with each other and with God as Jesus himself is one with God. In our passage here, we read of believers with great diversity of backgrounds and attitudes being built together into one holy temple of adoration, with Jesus as the keystone. In tomorrow's study we will see this vision expanded to cosmic proportions, as all creation is implicated in the work of reconciliation begun by Jesus on the cross and entrusted to us in building, through his Spirit, the peaceable kingdom.

The process of reconciliation is the great work of the kingdom of God. In the beginning, God created all things, blessed them and pronounced them good. Creation was diversity within unity, streaming forth from the word of God who is three in one. From the fall of Adam and Eve, to the confounded speech of the Tower of Babel to the war-torn, ecologically destructive, poverty-scarred world of today, human sin has torn God's beautiful web of unity, bringing dissension and division. The cross of Jesus is the starting point for healing the whole of creation, drawing all people and all living beings back into an undivided holistic expression of the love of God. In building the kingdom we join God's work of reconciliation, the healing of humanity and nature.

Watchpoint: 'Pick up the pieces so that nothing may be lost' (John 6:12, paraphrased).

Prayer

Loving God, help me to work towards wholeness. Where I see people feeling and expressing enmity, help me to sow seeds of peace. Where I feel dislike or distrust, help me to choose kindness and understanding.

PENELOPE WILCOCK

COLOSSIANS 1:15–20 (NIV, ABRIDGED)

The well-being of all creation

The Son is the image of the invisible God, the firstborn over all creation. For in him all things were created: things in heaven and on earth, visible and invisible, whether thrones or powers or rulers or authorities... He is before all things, and in him all things hold together... For God was pleased to have all his fullness dwell in him, and through him to reconcile to himself all things, whether things on earth or things in heaven, by making peace through his blood, shed on the cross.

You would think, to listen to some people talk, that the human race was the only species God had time for. As 18th-century Enlightenment thought influenced scientists, then wider society, then the clergy, then the whole church, it imported a misunderstanding that only humanity was, in the truest sense, alive. We came to believe that other living beings were little more than machines, there for our use and pleasure and nothing else. That, however, was not always the Christian perspective on creation. Our word 'animal' comes directly from the Latin word for 'soul'. The story of Noah speaks of God entering a covenant relationship with every living being (Genesis 9:8–17): this would not be possible if they had no soul dimension.

God created the earth, entered a covenant relationship with his creation and, in the cross of Jesus, reaches out to save creation from the thrall of sin and death (Romans 8:18–22). God was in Jesus, re-establishing the pattern shattered by human sin, not only for the salvation of the human race but also to redeem the entire cosmos. When we work to build God's kingdom on earth, we accept our ancient responsibility as stewards of creation, playing our part in the work of the restoration and protection of the well-being of it all, not just the human species.

Watchpoint: Thy kingdom come on earth as it is in heaven.

Prayer

Creator God, grant me the grace to be a faithful steward of the creation you have pronounced good. May my everyday choices reflect the greater dimension of this noble calling, to protect the well-being of this beautiful blue planet that you made and love.

PENELOPE WILCOCK

The Holy Spirit

When the day of Pentecost came, they were all together in one place. Suddenly a sound like the blowing of a violent wind came from heaven and filled the whole house where they were sitting. They saw what seemed to be tongues of fire that separated and came to rest on each of them. All of them were filled with the Holy Spirit and began to speak in other tongues as the Spirit enabled them.

When the disciples meet to pray, the fire of God descends. It is the power of his Spirit, dividing so that it comes to rest on every head individually. The coming of the Spirit is not a group or organisational thing only, but a matter of powerful personal experience.

Each one of us, too, plays our own personal and individual part in bringing in the kingdom; it can never be simply left to someone else.

It does not stop there, though. Those separated tongues of fire enable understanding and communication. When the disciples prayed and praised as the Spirit gave them utterance, they could be understood by people from whom they would normally be divided by language. The miracle draws us together as one human family, overcoming our alienation. There are no foreigners in the kingdom of God. The fire of God's power is love. Resting on us, it kindles the passion of each individual heart and this becomes the bond of our belonging. We are the living stones built together into a temple for the praise of God (1 Peter 2:5).

The kingdom originates with inspiration and is expressed in organisation—not the dry, mechanistic organisation of mere structures and procedures, the expression of human planning, but the organic arising of holy community. The Spirit at work in each of us joins us all together.

Watchword: '"Not by might nor by power, but by my Spirit," says the Lord Almighty' (Zechariah 4:6).

Prayer

Spirit of God, fall afresh on me, fill me with your love and power, lead me in your way. Help me to take my place in your family, your household of faith. By your grace at work in my life, may I learn to love my neighbour as myself.

PENELOPE WILCOCK

Bible stories rediscovered: Gideon

Much of the book of Judges is uncomfortable to modern ears. Punctuated by abhorrent violence, it records some of the darkest days of Israel's rebellion. On one level it is a history book, chronicling a particularly chaotic period between the death of Joshua and the first kings. It is also, however, a rich account of God's dealings with his people in which God's enduring patience and boundless grace are highlighted again and again. Throughout Judges we find a recurring sequence of rebellion, repentance, rescue and rest as Israel succumbs to the enticements of Canaanite idolatry, is brought to her knees by the consequences and is rescued once again by an ever-merciful Yahweh. As this vicious circle begins its fourth cycle, we meet Gideon.

We meet him at a time of great tension. There is a prevailing climate of terror. Midianite marauders are expected any moment. Israel is worn down by successive invasions, starving as crops and livestock are plundered year after year. The nation is desperate for a leader, a saviour, but who in their right mind would assume such a role at a time like this?

Then we find ourselves watching a young man. Partially hidden by an oak tree are two troughs, hewn out of rock: an upper one for trampling the grapes and a lower one for collecting their juice. Here is Gideon, clandestinely threshing wheat, hiding from Midianite eyes and wondering what will become of Israel.

So begins an account comprising two inextricably intertwined stories. The first story traces the life and experiences of an ordinary young man. We see how God nurtures and stretches Gideon's faith, taking a diffident and somewhat confused lad and transforming him into a leader who would radically alter the plight of a nation. The second story traces God's compassionate intervention in the life of Israel as they alternately battle against and yield to the temptation to forget their God and adopt the morals and deities of their powerful neighbours.

More than three millennia later, the challenges that brought fear into the heart of Gideon and the temptations that enticed Israel remain, but so, fortunately, does the indisputable hero of both stories, for it is none other than YHWH, the Lord God, himself.

Steve Aisthorpe

JUDGES 6:1–5 (NIV, ABRIDGED)

Calamitous consequences

The Israelites did evil in the eyes of the Lord, and for seven years he gave them into the hands of the Midianites. Because the power of Midian was so oppressive, the Israelites prepared shelters for themselves in mountain clefts, caves and strongholds. Whenever the Israelites planted their crops, the Midianites, Amalekites and other eastern peoples invaded the country. They... ruined the crops all the way to Gaza and did not spare a living thing for Israel, neither sheep nor cattle nor donkeys. They came up with their livestock and their tents like swarms of locusts. It was impossible to count them or their camels; they invaded the land to ravage it.

I remember bringing the note home from school. I was 13 and, if parental consent was given, would watch a film about the dropping of the atomic bomb on Hiroshima. Horrific images from that film are etched in my mind still. There is regular media debate about whether past atrocities are best forgotten or whether every generation needs reminders.

For Israel, for generations to come, mention of 'Midian' would evoke chilling recollections of the consequences of treating YHWH with contempt—and assure them of his abundant mercy and his incomparable power (Isaiah 9:4). Swarms of locusts can cover hundreds of square miles, bringing a tidal wave of devastation. This was an appropriate simile for the Midianites, with their vast numbers and ruthless 'scorched earth' policy. Their camels were the long-range missiles of the ancient east, enabling raids to be mounted across huge tracts of waterless wilderness.

Again and again, the famished, terrified Israelites cowered in rocky crevices. Season after season, Midianite livestock gorged on the crops of the Israelites, the fruit of their arduous labour. Through their own poor choices, the Israelites had sacrificed the prosperity and security promised to their forefathers and reaped the consequences of their rebellion and blatant disobedience (see Deuteronomy 28). Surely now they would wake up to the foolishness of doing the very thing that YHWH had forbidden (Judges 6:10)?

Reflection

Is there a past lesson, learned from our God, that you need to recall today?

STEVE AISTHORPE

Divine perspective

When the Israelites cried out to the Lord because of Midian, he sent them a prophet, who said, 'This is what the Lord, the God of Israel, says: I brought you up out of Egypt... I said to you, "I am the Lord your God; do not worship the gods of the Amorites, in whose land you live." But you have not listened to me.' The angel of the Lord came and sat down under the oak in Ophrah that belonged to Joash the Abiezrite, where his son Gideon was threshing wheat in a winepress to keep it from the Midianites. When the angel of the Lord appeared to Gideon, he said, 'The Lord is with you, mighty warrior.' 'Pardon me, my lord,' Gideon replied, 'but if the Lord is with us, why has all this happened to us?'

Like the prodigal son who 'came to his senses' (Luke 15:17) after craving a mouthful of pig swill, the Israelites finally woke up to the grim reality of their situation. Hungry, frightened, locked into a vicious circle of humanitarian crises, they urgently needed a divine perspective—and the Lord responded through an anonymous messenger.

The prophet's stark accusation (Judges 6:8–10) brought home a devastating realisation: they had neglected the first commandment (Exodus 20:1–4). Once again, the oft-repeated sequence had run its course—obedience had led to a season of peace (Judges 5:31); there had been a gradual slide into complacency and idolatry; then, finally, a season of harsh oppression had caused them to cry out to the Lord.

The prophet's indictment seems to stop in mid-flow. Instead of pronouncing a verdict, the scene suddenly shifts to a wine press, where a young man is hiding, secretly threshing wheat. He may be hidden from murderous Midianite eyes, but his position is wide open to 'the Angel of YHWH'. Believing his people to be abandoned by their God (Judges 6:13), he, too, needed a revelation of God's perspective. Just as Jesus revealed to Peter who he would become (Matthew 16:17–18), so the angel addressed Gideon as the one he would become in the hands of God's Spirit: 'mighty warrior'.

Prayer

All-knowing Father, please give me a glimpse of your perspective today.

STEVE AISTHORPE

The ultimate promise

The Lord turned to him and said, 'Go in the strength you have and save Israel out of Midian's hand. Am I not sending you?' 'Pardon me, my lord,' Gideon replied, 'but how can I save Israel? My clan is the weakest in Manasseh, and I am the least in my family.' The Lord answered, 'I will be with you, and you will strike down all the Midianites together.'

Some years ago, while climbing in the Alps, I was caught off guard by a sudden electrical storm. My friend and I began a rapid retreat. As lightning flashed all around and the air crackled with static, I was terrified. Then I recalled some words from Isaiah that I had been trying to memorise: 'When you pass through the waters, I will be with you… When you walk through the fire, you will not be burned' (Isaiah 43:2). Remembering them in that moment, trusting that the God who controls the elemental forces of the universe is also the one who says, 'Do not be afraid, for I am with you' (Isaiah 43:5), I experienced a deep peace.

Presented with 'mission impossible' ('Go… save Israel out of Midian's hand' (Judges 6:14), Gideon needed reassurance—lots of reassurance. As an Israelite living a millennium before Christ, Gideon had no doubts about the awesome power and splendid majesty of God. His name was too sacred to pass their lips. His utter holiness evoked the deepest reverence imaginable. No wonder Gideon fully expected to die after seeing 'the angel of the Lord face to face' (vv. 22–23). However, while Gideon had no qualms about God's incomparable might, like Moses before him (Exodus 3:12), he needed considerable reassurance that the all-powerful YHWH was going to be with him.

Throughout the whole Bible account, the Lord's definitive promise, his ultimate pledge of victory, his final word in the face of the most colossal challenges—is to say, simply and categorically, 'I will be with you.' If that seems inadequate, then perhaps, in the provocative words of the title of a challenging book by J.B. Phillips, 'Your God is too small'.

'Reflection

Consider afresh just who it is who promises you, 'I am with you always'
(Matthew 28:20).

STEVE AISTHORPE

Revelation, recognition... and worship

Gideon replied, 'If now I have found favour in your eyes, give me a sign that it is really you talking to me. Please do not go away until I come back and bring my offering and set it before you.' And the Lord said, 'I will wait until you return.' Gideon went inside, prepared a young goat, and from an ephah of flour he made bread without yeast. Putting the meat in a basket and its broth in a pot, he brought them out and offered them to him under the oak... With the tip of the staff that was in his hand, the angel of the Lord touched the meat and the unleavened bread. Fire flared from the rock, consuming the meat and the bread. And the angel of the Lord disappeared. When Gideon realised that it was the angel of the Lord, he exclaimed, 'Ah, Sovereign Lord! I have seen the angel of the Lord face to face!'

The phrase 'Life is a journey' is in such common usage that it is in danger of becoming a threadbare cliché. Yet the metaphor of a journey is helpful and goes back to the very roots of our Christian heritage. From the literal journeys of Abraham and Moses, through the writings of spiritual guides such as John of the Cross and Teresa of Avila, to modern theories of faith development, there is a clear consensus that we are on a journey of discovery regarding who God is and who we are. Indeed, the two are inextricably intertwined into a single journey.

When we meet Gideon under the oak tree, the trajectory and tempo of his journey are undergoing a fundamental transformation. Within a few verses a pattern emerges that is common to all our Christian lives. God reveals himself; Gideon recognises his holy presence and responds in worship. In that worship there is an encounter that transcends the ordinary and propels him into fresh acts of obedience. Gideon's language gives insight into his spiritual progress. His eyes are opened as he moves from a merely respectful 'lord' (v. 13) to a reverential 'Lord' (v. 13) to an almost breathless, awed 'Ah, Sovereign Lord!' (v. 22).

Prayer

Open my eyes, Lord. Amen

STEVE AISTHORPE

From idolatry to integrity

That same night the Lord said to him, 'Take the second bull from your father's herd, the one seven years old. Tear down your father's altar to Baal and cut down the Asherah pole beside it. Then build a proper kind of altar to the Lord your God on the top of this height. Using the wood of the Asherah pole that you cut down, offer the second bull as a burnt offering.' So Gideon took ten of his servants and did as the Lord told him. But because he was afraid of his family and the townspeople, he did it at night rather than in the daytime.

A Scottish friend working abroad used to delight in wearing a T-shirt bearing the words, 'You can take the boy out of Scotland, but you can't take Scotland out of the boy.' As Yahweh seeks to turn the nation from idolatry to integrity, he needs to purge them of deep-seated Canaanite influences, to 'take Canaan out of the boy'. Gideon also needs to discover that radical obedience is not a perilous gamble.

'Pick and mix religion' had become the norm in Ophrah. Reverence for YHWH had been merged with the veneration of Canaanite gods. Gideon had already made him an offering (v. 20) and constructed an altar (v. 24), but now YHWH requests his singular allegiance. The cult of Baal and the way of Yahweh are mutually exclusive and Gideon must eradicate the symbols of idolatry, sacrificing them to the Lord. The fact that Gideon's bold act is executed in trepidation and darkness reminds us that we are called to be faithful but not necessarily heroic.

God's call to uproot all that undermines our single-minded adherence to him is one for all generations. Writing to Christians scattered throughout the world, James coined a new word to challenge his readers to unadulterated devotion to Jesus Christ. The word he used to describe people attempting to follow Christ while continuing to embrace contradictory values is often translated as 'double-minded' (James 1:8; 4:8), but literally means 'divided-soul'. It highlights the ludicrous impossibility of being committed to two different ways.

Reflection

'Create in me a clean heart, O God. Renew a loyal spirit within me'
(Psalm 51:10, NLT).

STEVE AISTHORPE

Additional assurance

Now all the Midianites, Amalekites and other eastern peoples joined forces and crossed over the Jordan and camped in the Valley of Jezreel. Then the Spirit of the Lord came on Gideon, and he blew a trumpet, summoning the Abiezrites to follow him. He sent messengers throughout Manasseh, calling them to arms, and also into Asher, Zebulun and Naphtali, so that they too went up to meet them. Gideon said to God, 'If you will save Israel by my hand as you have promised—look, I will place a wool fleece on the threshing-floor. If there is dew only on the fleece and all the ground is dry, then I will know that you will save Israel by my hand, as you said.'

Working as a guide, helping people to achieve their mountaineering ambitions, I learned the powerful impact of a gentle but firm pull on the rope. It was amazing to see the confidence-inspiring effect as a person was reminded that they were in safe hands and help was nearby if needed. The intention was never to drag them physically up the climb; it was more of an occasional taut rope than a serious tug. When courage was ebbing or strength waning, a simple reminder of their security was often all that was needed to stimulate renewed effort and encourage fresh focus.

Throughout the account of God's dealings with Gideon, we find again and again that God understands his frailty and delights in encouraging and enabling him. Earlier we noted that Gideon was fearful but still obedient. In today's passage we find that he is hesitant but earnest and not unbelieving. It is impossible for us to comprehend the enormity of the undertaking that had been assigned to Gideon. We should not read into his prayerful laying out of the fleece a lack of faith. In fact, we should note his candid belief that God had spoken (vv. 36–37). How encouraging, though, to observe that the Lord is not only almighty and all-knowing but also gracious and willing tenderly to reassure and strengthen his servant.

Reflection

When our sincere desire is to be faithful to our Lord, he will not despise a genuine request for assurance and assistance.

STEVE AISTHORPE

JUDGES 7:1–5 (TNIV, ABRIDGED)

When less is more

Early in the morning, Jerub-Baal (that is, Gideon) and all his men camped at the spring of Harod. The camp of Midian was north of them in the valley near the hill of Moreh. The Lord said to Gideon, 'You have too many men. I cannot deliver Midian into their hands, or Israel would boast against me, "My own strength has saved me." Now announce to the army, "Anyone who trembles with fear may turn back and leave Mount Gilead."' So twenty-two thousand men left, while ten thousand remained. But the Lord said to Gideon, 'There are still too many men. Take them down to the water, and I will sift them out for you there.'... So Gideon took the men down to the water. There the Lord told him, 'Separate those who lap the water with their tongues like a dog from those who kneel down to drink.'

As if perched on a nearby hilltop, we are given a bird's-eye view of the action. It seems that Gideon's preparation is over. When the angel of the Lord addressed him as 'mighty hero' (6:12), it seemed almost laughable. Now he leads thousands into battle. It is a rousing sight. The Israelites have emerged from their caves and strongholds (6:2) to confront their oppressors. However, a glance to the north reveals the seething throngs of the formidable Midianite war machine. The outcome seems inevitable. Years of oppression and starvation will end in a bloodbath on the battlefield. As the massed armies gather for the violent climax of years of repression, however, something bizarre and totally illogical begins to unfold.

Some commentators have interpreted God's reduction of the Israelite army in terms of strategy and logic. Sending the faint-hearted home was already considered best practice, so that others would not become disheartened (Deuteronomy 20:8). Various rational explanations have been given, too, for why those who lapped water showed themselves to be better soldiers, but such justifications miss the point. Gideon was not recruiting a small squad of crack troops. Rather, he needed to be sure never to think, 'My own strength has saved me' (Judges 7:2).

Reflection
'My power works best in weakness' (2 Corinthians 12:9).

STEVE AISTHORPE

JUDGES 7:8–14 (NIV, ABRIDGED)

Encouragement in unlikely places

Now the camp of Midian lay below [Gideon] in the valley. During that night the Lord said to Gideon, 'Get up, go down against the camp, because I am going to give it into your hands. If you are afraid to attack, go down to the camp with your servant Purah and listen to what they are saying…' Gideon arrived just as a man was telling a friend his dream. 'I had a dream,' he was saying. 'A round loaf of barley bread came tumbling into the Midianite camp. It struck the tent with such force that the tent overturned and collapsed.' His friend responded, 'This can be nothing other than the sword of Gideon son of Joash, the Israelite. God has given the Midianites and the whole camp into his hands.'

The words 'If you are afraid' remind us of God's intimate knowledge of Gideon, and the encouragement he provides demonstrates his flawless provision. Time and again, Gideon is challenged by daunting tasks and then enabled through God's timely and fitting guidance or reassurance.

It was US President Franklin D. Roosevelt who, in his inaugural speech in 1933, stated, 'The only thing we have to fear is fear itself.' At first his bold statement seems paradoxical, but he was making an important observation. Fear has the potential to paralyse or propel us into panic. While most in the animal kingdom have a programmed response to fear that has been termed 'flight or fight', the mature human has the potential to evaluate fearful situations and make a considered response.

When faced with fear, we do well to 'tune in' consciously to what God might be saying. Is this fear a warning to be heeded or a trial to be overcome in his strength? If it is the latter, we should be open to receiving encouragement—sometimes from unexpected places.

Gideon has come a long way since we first met him cowering in the winepress. Each step of obedience has brought a further endowment of courage as he has experienced God's faithfulness.

Prayer
Lord, help me to know when anxiety indicates danger to be avoided and when it is a trial to be overcome with your help. Amen

STEVE AISTHORPE

JUDGES 7:15–18 (NIV, ABRIDGED)

Faith turns to action

When Gideon heard the dream and its interpretation, he bowed down and worshipped. He returned to the camp of Israel and called out, 'Get up! The Lord has given the Midianite camp into your hands.' Dividing the three hundred men into three companies, he placed trumpets and empty jars in the hands of all of them, with torches inside. 'Watch me,' he told them. 'Follow my lead... When I and all who are with me blow our trumpets, then from all round the camp blow yours and shout, "For the Lord and for Gideon."'

Encouraged by the words of an anonymous enemy, Gideon is utterly convinced that God can give them victory against their enemies. Perhaps more accurately, he realises that God himself can be victorious through their obedience. It is a conviction he is prepared to stake his life on—and the lives of his bravest troops: 'Get up! The Lord has given the Midianite camp into your hands' (v. 15).

Believing is one thing. Stepping out in faith when totally outnumbered and outgunned—a handful of unarmed men against the military might of the Midianites—is another thing entirely. This is where faith ceases to be a noun only and needs to become a verb. An interesting story comes to mind on this subject.

In 1859 Jean-François Gravelet, better known as 'Blondin', crossed the gorge below the Niagara Falls by tightrope. He performed the feat on several later occasions, often adding new elements of difficulty. History records that, on one occasion, Blondin asked the crowd if they believed he could cross the tightrope while pushing a wheelbarrow. Having already seen him cross the wire with apparent ease and having heard about his amazing stunts, they responded with unanimous support, 'Yes, you can do it!' Blondin was ready to attempt this amazing feat, but before he set out on the rope, he had one last question for the crowd: 'Which of you will ride in the wheelbarrow?' The crowd fell silent. Their faith in him was apparently resolute... but only in theory!

Reflection
'Faith: if it is alone and includes no actions, then it is dead'
(James 2:17, GNB).

STEVE AISTHORPE

A tense situation defused

Now the Ephraimites asked Gideon, 'Why have you treated us like this? Why didn't you call us when you went to fight Midian?' And they challenged him vigorously. But he answered them, 'What have I accomplished compared to you? Aren't the gleanings of Ephraim's grapes better than the full grape harvest of Abiezer? God gave Oreb and Zeeb, the Midianite leaders, into your hands. What was I able to do compared to you?' At this, their resentment against him subsided.

Gideon's extraordinary routing of the Midiantites was inexplicable in terms of military strategy and its lessons would not be lost on future generations. No doubt it was an event that Asa had in mind as he called out to the Lord, 'O Lord, no one but you can help the powerless against the mighty! Help us, O Lord our God, for we trust in you alone' (2 Chronicles 14:11, NLT). Perhaps it was in the thoughts of Solomon as he wrote his proverb, 'The wicked flee though no one pursues, but the righteous are as bold as a lion' (Proverbs 28:1). However, with the tables now well and truly turned and the Midianites fleeing in disarray, there is one tribe that chooses this of all moments to express a grievance. The Ephraimites are vexed that they had not taken a prominent role in the game-changing events. This is a tribe that had developed a prima donna attitude; an overestimated sense of its own importance.

Clearly Gideon does not believe that this is the time to confront a furious ally. In order to preserve their alliance and complete the mission, he chooses a diplomatic option. Perhaps remembering how his father's wise words had quenched the wrath of the villagers of Ophrah (Judges 6:31), Gideon demonstrates the truth that 'a gentle answer turns away wrath' (Proverbs 15:1). With the benefit of hindsight, however, while it seems wise to have avoided a confrontation at such a crucial time, it is also worth noting that the Ephraimites' unchecked pride and their unchallenged contentious attitude would only grow and fester until dealt with by others some years later (12:1–6).

Reflection

There is a right time to shut up and another to speak up (Ecclesiastes 3:7).

STEVE AISTHORPE

A test of character

Gideon and his three hundred men, exhausted yet keeping up the pursuit, came to the Jordan and crossed it. He said to the men of Sukkoth, 'Give my troops some bread; they are worn out, and I am still pursuing Zebah and Zalmunna, the kings of Midian.' But the officials of Sukkoth said, 'Do you already have the hands of Zebah and Zalmunna in your possession? Why should we give bread to your troops?' Then Gideon replied, 'Just for that, when the Lord has given Zebah and Zalmunna into my hand, I will tear your flesh with desert thorns and briers.'

Hebrews 11:32 records Gideon as a hero of faith, and he shows an earnest desire to follow the Lord, but we now meet him at the end of his tether. After days of anxiety, sleep deprivation and physical exertion, 'They were bone-tired but still pressing the pursuit' (Judges 8:4, THE MESSAGE). Gideon was in just the kind of situation in which we all find ourselves from time to time—weary, our patience exhausted, yet faced with some trivial irritation that stands between us and where we want to be.

Gideon has undertaken breathtaking acts of courage, excelled as a leader and demonstrated an unswerving faith in God. Yet it is perhaps now that he faces his toughest test of character: exhilarated by an astonishing victory, the man of the hour, how will he respond to people who stand in his way? Yes, hospitality was a sacred duty in the ancient East, but the people of Succoth and Paniel, unsure of the final outcome of the conflict, were probably terrified of the horrific retaliation with which the Midianites would reward any who helped Gideon and his men.

Gideon, as good as his word (Judges 8:13–21), returned from victory to mete out a merciless vengeance on those who had refused support. Hints of personal vendettas and the mass slaughters that went well beyond the original threat and exceeded any sense of proportionality point to troubling developments in Gideon's character and challenge us about our own. When we are tired, hungry, frustrated, how do we cope with the annoyances that cross our path?

Prayer

Lord, please increase my patience. Amen

STEVE AISTHORPE

Humble words, proud actions

The Israelites said to Gideon, 'Rule over us—you, your son and your grandson—because you have saved us from the hand of Midian.' But Gideon told them, 'I will not rule over you, nor will my son rule over you. The Lord will rule over you.' And he said, 'I do have one request, that each of you give me an earring from your share of the plunder.' (It was the custom of the Ishmaelites to wear gold earrings.)... Gideon made the gold into an ephod, which he placed in Ophrah, his town. All Israel prostituted themselves by worshipping it there, and it became a snare to Gideon and his family.

We open the newspaper and, each time, our hearts sink as we reflect on how such a promising start ended in scandal, disgrace or discredit. Year on year, our media reveals that sporting heroes have been cheating, prominent politicians have been duplicitous and corporate executives have allowed greed to undermine their integrity. Too few, it seems, can end their days with Paul's bold testimony: 'I have fought the good fight, I have finished the race, I have kept the faith' (2 Timothy 4:7).

What about Gideon? He had been acutely aware of the danger of attributing Israel's salvation to anyone other than the Lord himself (Judges 7:2). It takes inordinate strength of character, however, to remain unmoved by acclamations and a request to accept a prominent and privileged position. Will he be able to retain the right perspective of the Lord as saviour and himself as a humble servant?

When taken in isolation, his response to the request for him and his descendants to rule over the nation is encouraging (8:23), but his next actions suggest that Gideon has been seduced by pride. Gathering plundered gold to create a duplicate of the high priest's sacred garment and instrument of discerning God's will (Exodus 28:6–14) creates a stumbling block for the Israelites with their propensity for idolatry. Our worst fears are confirmed when one of Gideon's sons is called Abimelech (Judges 8:31)—a name that means 'the king is my father'!

Reflection

'When pride comes, then comes disgrace, but with humility comes wisdom'
(Proverbs 11:2).

STEVE AISTHORPE

Glory years... but not for long

Thus Midian was subdued before the Israelites and did not raise its head again. During Gideon's lifetime, the land had peace for forty years... No sooner had Gideon died than the Israelites again prostituted themselves to the Baals. They set up Baal-Berith as their god and did not remember the Lord their God, who had rescued them from the hands of all their enemies on every side. They also failed to show any loyalty to the family of Jerub-Baal (that is, Gideon) in spite of all the good things he had done for them.

What a contrast to when we first met Gideon. From constant fear and debilitating hunger under the devastating oppression of the Midianites, the Israelites had now been delighting in 40 years of peace. The Lord, constantly faithful, has done exactly what he promised (6:14). We soon learn, however, that what appears to be Gideon's glorious legacy is, in fact, shallow and tenuous—founded on faithfulness in the past, but fundamentally flawed by infidelity in the present.

Perhaps the dominant theme in the life of Gideon is weakness. In our earliest encounters with him he was 'weak' in ways that were obvious to all: he lacked confidence, experience and relevant skills. This, however, is a weakness that the Lord delights in, transforming and using it as a channel for his power. It is a precursor to the kind of adventures of faith for which Gideon is best known. Indeed, he is immortalised as one 'whose weakness was turned to strength' (Hebrews 11:34).

Unfortunately, the weakness that characterises the latter part of Gideon's life could not be more contradictory. This weakness is not a conduit for God's enabling and an instrument for his glory. Instead, it is rooted in pride and leads to idolatry, taking the nation away from simple dependency on the Lord. Just as Gideon demonstrated how the faithful actions of an individual can transform the fortunes of a nation for the better, he leaves us with the salutary lesson that the influence of individuals can be far-reaching in less positive and even toxic ways.

Prayer

Lord, please help us to not only deepen our trust in you but also sustain it to the very end. Amen

STEVE AISTHORPE

The call to ministry, as you are

This is the time of year when newly trained ordinands will be set apart by their churches for the work of ministry. It is an enormous step for them and one that is not undertaken lightly. It usually follows a lengthy period of discernment by both the individuals and the churches, then, of course, a period of rigorous training and preparation.

All of us are called to ministry in its broadest sense, in that we are all to serve the Lord wherever we are and through whatever we do. This kind of ministry is of equal value to what is sometimes termed 'full-time' ministry and, nowadays, the importance of serving God in the 'marketplace' is recognised and given greater prominence, as it should be. We must not overlook the fact, however, that God does call some people to lay aside their secular responsibilities and devote themselves fully to the task of Christian ministry in its various forms. This is a noble calling and one we will be exploring over the next two weeks, for several reasons.

First, to give encouragement to those who are entering Christian ministry or who already find themselves serving God in some full-time capacity. Second, to enable those who may be considering Christian vocation to think biblically about what is involved. Third, to stimulate those who do not have such a calling to understand and pray for those who do—your vicar or church leader, for example, a mission partner working overseas, a youth worker in your local town and so on.

The passages we will be looking at are, in the main, about the lives of the two great apostles Peter and Paul. In some ways they were very different, Peter having a focus on the Jewish world and Paul reaching out to the Gentiles. They had their moments of misunderstanding, too, over the radical nature of the gospel (Galatians 2:11–13), and Peter (like many of us) had to admit that he sometimes found Paul's writings hard to understand (2 Peter 3:16). What they had in common, though, was a passionate desire to follow Jesus and serve him, no matter what the cost.

We begin in the Old Testament, with the call of Jeremiah.

Tony Horsfall

The call of God

> The word of the Lord came to me, saying, 'Before I formed you in the womb I knew you, before you were born I set you apart; I appointed you as a prophet to the nations… See, today I appoint you over nations and kingdoms to uproot and to tear down, to destroy and overthrow, to build and to plant.'

Rightly understood, the call to ministry has its origin not in human desire but in the heart and mind of God. It is not us volunteering to serve God, but him setting us apart for the work he has for us to do. This awareness gives us our confidence when the going is tough.

The word of the Lord to Jeremiah highlights four actions of God in his life, three of which take place even before he was born and almost certainly without his conscious knowledge.

'I knew you': the starting point is God's plan and purpose and his knowledge of what he had in mind for Jeremiah to do. Like an architect who designs a building in line with its preconceived purpose, so the Creator God has made Jeremiah with his purpose in mind.

'I formed you': even in the womb Jeremiah was being shaped to fit his calling. His physical frame, mental capacity and personality are not afterthoughts or things of chance, but aspects of the detailed planning of God (Psalm 139:13–16).

'I set you apart': before he was actually born, the hand of God was upon his life. He, even then, had a destiny, a God-given purpose that he would eventually come to realise and grow into.

'I appointed you': now, in this moment of time ('today'), realisation dawns on the young man that he has been called by God. He feels unprepared for such a calling and afraid, but with the calling comes not only the spoken reassurance of God but also an affirming touch of grace. The God who calls is the God who enables.

To be called by God like this is an amazing privilege. What Jeremiah experienced, Peter and Paul experienced and so do men and women today.

Reflection
Known… formed… set apart… appointed.

TONY HORSFALL

Come and follow me

As Jesus was walking beside the Sea of Galilee, he saw two brothers, Simon called Peter and his brother Andrew. They were casting a net into the lake, for they were fishermen. 'Come, follow me,' Jesus said, 'and I will send you out to fish for people.' At once they left their nets and followed him.

A popular newspaper has, in its weekend supplement, a regular feature called 'The day that changed my life'. I enjoy reading the various stories of how different people, through unexpected events, suddenly found their lives changing dramatically. I guess Peter (at this point still known as Simon) could have written his own account of how an ordinary day proved to be a significant turning point in his life.

Simon and his brother Andrew were fishermen and they were content to make their living in a simple way, fishing on the Sea of Galilee. They were simple men, too, regarded by others as being 'unschooled, ordinary men' (Acts 4:13), happy to earn a basic level of pay by selling their catch, satisfied with their humdrum existence in rural Galilee. Then, one day, Jesus stepped into their lives and everything changed.

Matthew's account suggests that they made the life-changing decision to leave everything and follow him instantaneously, but, when we put the Gospel accounts of the call of the disciples together, there was probably more to it than this (Luke 5:1–11; John 1:40–42). Probably there had been several encounters with the new rabbi from Nazareth and perhaps they had been weighing up his teaching for a little while. At any rate, when the moment comes and Jesus issues an invitation to them to become his followers, they are ready to respond. They do so not in a superficial or half-hearted way, but with an all-out commitment.

Such is the impact that Jesus can make on our lives. He is looking for disciples, those who will take his teaching seriously and live it out in their daily lives, and, for some, the call to follow is, quite literally, a call to leave everything and set out on the adventure of faith. It is, indeed, a call to ministry.

Prayer
Lord, may I be ready to follow.

TONY HORSFALL

A new name and a new direction

> Andrew, Simon Peter's brother, was one of the two who heard what John had said and who had followed Jesus. The first thing Andrew did was to find his brother Simon and tell him, 'We have found the Messiah' (that is, the Christ). And he brought him to Jesus. Jesus looked at him and said, 'You are Simon son of John. You will be called Cephas' (which, when translated, is Peter).

The two brothers may have been ordinary men, but spiritually they were alive to God, and Andrew at least had been influenced by the revival preaching of John the Baptist. It is touching to see how he shares his newfound faith with his brother and brings him to Jesus.

Did this encounter precede the one by the lakeside? We cannot say, but we do know that it was part of the process by which Peter and his brother not only got to know Jesus but also sensed a call to follow him.

With typical discernment, Jesus looks straight into Peter's soul. He shows he is aware of his past, of his earthly identity, by addressing him as 'Simon son of John' (v. 42), but Peter's past is not what matters now and his human ancestry will no longer define him. By giving him a new name, Jesus gives him a heavenly identity, marking him out as someone who has a divine destiny, a part to play in the coming kingdom. How much Peter understood this or what he made of the name change, we do not know, but, during the months of following Jesus, he would experience a growing revelation of who Jesus was and a growing transformation within himself.

What we can conclude is that the call of Jesus always has the potential to liberate us from our own past, who we may once have been, and release us into a new identity as children of God. It also offers the possibility of a new direction in life, of following in the steps of our master.

The path to ministry often begins with a life-changing encounter with Jesus and it can happen to ordinary people doing ordinary things.

Prayer
Lord, meet me in the ordinariness of life.

TONY HORSFALL

Gripped by the truth

When Jesus came to the region of Caesarea Philippi, he asked his disciples, 'Who do people say the Son of Man is?' They replied, 'Some say John the Baptist; others say Elijah; and still others, Jeremiah or one of the prophets.' 'But what about you?' he asked. 'Who do you say I am?' Simon Peter answered, 'You are the Messiah, the Son of the living God.' Jesus replied, 'Blessed are you, Simon son of Jonah, for this was not revealed to you by flesh and blood, but by my Father in heaven.'

The small band of disciples had spent many months in the company of Jesus, listening to his teaching, seeing him at work, getting to know him intimately, but had they grasped his true identity? Now is the moment to test their spiritual progress and Jesus asks them the most personal and searching question: 'Who do you say I am?'

Peter is the first to respond—no doubt because of his extravert personality, but also because of a moment of true spiritual insight. The penny has dropped. Jesus is the long-awaited Messiah, the Christ, none other than the Son of God. Such a conviction is not the result of intellectual reasoning or personal cleverness, but the gift of God. This kind of spiritual knowing comes by revelation and is the work of the Spirit of God. Certainty like this becomes the foundation stone on which faith is built, the bedrock on which a life of discipleship can rest securely.

Anyone contemplating Christian ministry must have a firm foundation within them, a deep knowing of who Jesus is and what it means to be in relationship with him. Theological truth can never replace personal conviction, just as intellectual awareness is no substitute for the spiritual insight imparted by the Spirit.

Each of us must answer this question posed by Jesus: 'Who do you say I am?' There can be no fudging of the issue, no hiding behind the opinions of others. We must be able to answer with clarity and conviction, 'You are the Christ, the Son of the living God.' Ministry begins here.

Reflection
Is your faith resting on solid ground?

TONY HORSFALL

Feed my sheep

When they finished eating, Jesus said to Simon Peter, 'Simon son of John, do you love me more than these?' 'Yes, Lord,' he said, 'you know that I love you.' Jesus said, 'Feed my lambs.' Again Jesus said, 'Simon son of John, do you love me?' He answered, 'Yes, Lord, you know that I love you.' Jesus said, 'Take care of my sheep.' The third time he said to him, 'Simon son of John, do you love me?' Peter was hurt because Jesus asked him the third time, 'Do you love me?' He said, 'Lord, you know all things; you know that I love you.' Jesus said, 'Feed my sheep.'

The thrice-repeated questioning of Peter by Jesus seems to have been for the purpose of restoring his soul, each affirmation of love corresponding to one of his three denials (Mark 14:66–72).

The Wonderful Counsellor knows the importance of our facing up to failure and the healing power of being given a second chance. The church of Jesus Christ is not to be led by those who have no weakness, but by those who are deeply aware of their own shortcomings, yet have learned to live in the wonder of forgiving grace. Good shepherds must gently lead the lambs in their care.

There is more to this intense questioning. The probing of Jesus is designed to allow the love that exists in Peter's heart to rise to the surface, to bring the depth and reality of it into his own consciousness. It is not to make Jesus feel better, but to help Peter himself realise the intensity of the love he has for the Lord.

Why? Because love for Jesus is the only true motivation for Christian ministry. If Peter is to feed his lambs and take care of his sheep, he will need to be someone who loves Jesus deeply. This will not only make him compassionate towards those he leads but also help him to persevere in his calling when the going is tough. Love will motivate his actions, guide his decisions and make his service sustainable.

Prayer
Lord, may all my service spring from love for you.

TONY HORSFALL

Good shepherds

Be shepherds of God's flock that is under your care, serving as overseers—not because you must, but because you are willing, as God wants you to be; not greedy for money, but eager to serve; not lording it over those entrusted to you, but being examples to the flock. And when the Chief Shepherd appears, you will receive the crown of glory that will never fade away.

By the time Peter is writing his epistles, he has been serving Christ for many years and therefore has much experience to reflect on. The metaphor of ministry as caring for the flock of God and the minister as a shepherd still dominates his thinking. His desire is that other leaders should share similar values.

At the heart of his understanding of leadership is that it is a way of serving people. Leaders must be first and foremost servants of God who use their gifts and abilities to serve his church. They take on the responsibility of leadership not as an obligation but with a joyful sense of calling. They work hard at the task, not simply for financial reward, but because of their enthusiasm for the work of God. Their motivation is to glorify the Lord.

This means that their leadership style is not one of lording it over people. They are not motivated by the desire for status or position, nor are they corrupted by power. Because they are servant-hearted people, they can exercise the authority inherent in any leadership role with humility and grace, seeking to empower others rather than dominate them. In this way, they become examples for their flock, modelling by their words and actions what it means to be a follower of Jesus. They anticipate their ultimate reward not in this life, but when Jesus returns.

Such leaders should never be taken for granted, nor taken advantage of by those whom they serve. Indeed, a congregation has a biblical responsibility prayerfully and practically to support those in leadership so that their work is a joy (1 Timothy 5:17–20; Hebrews 13:17).

Prayer
Lord, bless your church with servant-leaders; help us to love and encourage them.

TONY HORSFALL

The chief of sinners

I thank Christ Jesus our Lord, who has given me strength, that he considered me faithful, appointing me to his service. Even though I was once a blasphemer and a persecutor and a violent man, I was shown mercy because I acted in ignorance and unbelief. The grace of our Lord Jesus was poured out on me abundantly, along with the faith and love that are in Christ Jesus. Here is a trustworthy saying that deserves full acceptance: Christ Jesus came into the world to save sinners—of whom I am the worst.

Our attention turns now to the story of the apostle Paul. We are at once reminded of the life he lived as Saul of Tarsus—the proud Pharisee implacably opposed to the followers of Jesus and committed to their destruction. His conversion after being confronted by the risen Christ is graphically described in Acts 9:1–19, the backdrop to this passage.

Such a dramatic turnaround can only be understood as an act of grace. As we saw with Jeremiah, the purpose of God for a person's life reaches back into eternity and Paul is deeply aware of having been chosen by God. Only divine intervention can account for his change of heart and transformation from persecutor to preacher. Notice the key words describing God's activity in his life. He has been shown mercy; grace has been poured out upon him; faith and love have been formed in his heart. Here are the hallmarks of a genuine conversion and Paul is convinced that if he can be saved, anyone can.

If Peter carried within him a deep conviction concerning the identity of Jesus (the Christ, the Son of the living God), Paul had within him an absolute assurance of the power of Jesus to save sinners. This came from his personal experience and formed the bedrock of his ministry, shaping the way he approached his calling and motivating him into a life of ceaseless evangelism.

Each of us carries within us a 'life message', too—something that sums up our personal experience of Christ. It is what we know with most certainty, what we can share with most authority.

Reflection

What is your life message?

TONY HORSFALL

EPHESIANS 3:7–8, 12–13 (NIV 1984)

Ministry as gift

I became a servant of this gospel by the gift of God's grace given me through the working of his power. Although I am less than the least of all God's people, this grace was given me: to preach to the Gentiles the unsearchable riches of Christ... In him and through faith in him we may approach God with freedom and confidence. I ask you, therefore, not to be discouraged because of my sufferings for you, which are your glory.

As far as Paul was concerned, ministry was not a duty or an obligation, but a privilege, even when it involved suffering. Such was the deep sense of grace and gratitude that gripped his heart, for him to be called to serve Christ was the highest honour.

Of course he never forgot his history as blasphemer, persecutor and violent man, but it was not his past that defined him, even if it kept him humble. Nor was it the need to make amends that motivated him. A stronger power was at work within him—the power of God—and a better vision inspired him—that of sharing with those who had never heard 'the unsearchable riches of Christ' (v. 8).

To Paul more than to any other was given the understanding of what God had accomplished at the cross through Jesus, and his great joy was to help others see all that is available through the gospel.

In essence, the good news is this: by believing in Jesus, anyone, whether Jew or Gentile, can now approach God with freedom and confidence. In other words, we can know God and relate to him personally. The Church exists for one purpose and one purpose only: to declare this wisdom of God, to make the way of salvation clear and plain so everyone can understand. This was what Paul lived for and, in this sense, he became a servant of the gospel.

It is easy, in among the demands of church life and ministry in general, to lose sight of this, even when it is our core purpose. Sometimes we have to pause and bring ourselves back to what is the primary thing: to preach the unsearchable riches of Christ.

Reflection
To serve is a privilege.

TONY HORSFALL

1 CORINTHIANS 15:9–10 (NIV)

The grace that enables

For I am the least of the apostles and do not even deserve to be called an apostle, because I persecuted the church of God. But by the grace of God I am what I am, and his grace to me was not without effect. No, I worked harder than all of them—yet not I, but the grace of God that was with me.

It is easy to approach Christian ministry in the same way as we approach anything else—trying our best and working our hardest. If there is one important lesson to learn in Christian ministry, however, it is this: it cannot be done through human strength alone. Sometimes we can only understand this the hard way—by experiencing exhaustion, disillusionment, even burnout.

Paul was naturally an ambitious person, given to working hard to achieve his objectives. The way he threw himself wholeheartedly into destroying the fledgling church suggests a driven personality. It would have been easy for him to have brought that same human dynamism into his ministry. Indeed, given his history as a persecutor, it would not be surprising if he had sought to atone for his previous mistakes by immersing himself in his work. What is more, as a rather unusual and late addition to the apostolic circle, he might well have been tempted to prove himself by achieving more than the others.

Fortunately, he seems to have avoided these pitfalls and learned early the secret of the 'exchanged life'—that it is 'not I but the grace of God' (compare with Galatians 2:20). What this means is that, although we work hard, we are not to work out of our own energy, but with the energy and power that God gives to us. Grace, in this sense, is the power of God at work in us, enabling us to fulfil our calling and do the things that God asks of us. To understand this further, see Colossians 1:28–29 and Philippians 2:12–13.

How does this happen in practice? Through a deep-seated sense of dependency on God, a realisation that we cannot do it by ourselves and a prayerful, daily asking for his help.

Reflection
Not I, but Christ.

TONY HORSFALL

1 Corinthians 2:1–5 (NIV 1984)

Human weakness and divine power

When I came to you, brothers and sisters, I did not come with eloquence or superior wisdom as I proclaimed to you the testimony about God. For I resolved to know nothing while I was with you except Jesus Christ and him crucified. I came to you in weakness and fear, and with much trembling. My message and my preaching were not with wise and persuasive words, but with a demonstration of the Spirit's power, so that your faith might not rest on human wisdom, but on God's power.

The sense of dependency on God that we spoke about yesterday is illustrated again as Paul describes his ministry in Corinth. He did not approach the challenge of bringing the gospel to this godless city in a show of strength or human bravado. He did not demonstrate a 'can do' mentality or trust his considerable training or intellectual ability. He did not depend on his strong personality or eloquence. On the contrary, he came in weakness and fear and with much trembling.

Perhaps we imagine Paul as being self-confident and assertive, a 'strong, natural leader' who carried all before him. Perhaps we think, too, that Christian leaders should be like that, competent and assured, capable and triumphant. When we find that we do not match up to this ideal, we may be tempted to despair. That is why Paul's honest description of his own struggles not only gives us hope but also reveals to us that Christian ministry works best through human weakness.

Because of his sense of inadequacy, Paul depended on the power of the Spirit and so his words were not clothed with human wisdom but came anointed with God's authority. This meant that those who believed were basing their confidence not in Paul's wisdom, but on the power of God that was so evidently working through him.

There is always a temptation to despise our weakness and want to be rid of it, but the way of God is for us to become more dependent on him, more open to the work of his Spirit within us and more trusting that he can use us as we are.

Prayer
Holy Spirit of God, fall on me afresh.

Tony Horsfall

1 Corinthians 3:5–9 (NIV)

Ministry as partnership

What, after all, is Apollos? And what is Paul? Only servants, through whom you came to believe—as the Lord has assigned to each his task. I planted the seed, Apollos watered it, but God has been making it grow. So neither the one who plants nor the one who waters is anything, but only God, who makes things grow. The one who plants and the one who waters have one purpose, and they will each be rewarded according to their own labour. For we are fellow workers in God's service; you are God's field, God's building.

Ministry is about teamwork rather than individual accomplishment. Together we can achieve more than the sum total of our individual efforts. This is called 'synergy' and is at the heart of effective Christian service. Although the church in Corinth was dangerously focused on individuals (1:10–12), Paul was aware that he and Apollos were not rivals but partners in ministry, each having a particular, God-assigned job to do. Paul's ministry was to plant the seed of the gospel (get the church started), the ministry of Apollos to water it (develop it further). Their work was complementary and each was incomplete without the other.

At the same time, both Paul and Apollos were dependent on God to supply the essential ingredient, which was growth. Not only were they partners with each other, but, more importantly, they were partners with God: 'we are God's fellow-workers' (3:9).

It is vital to recognise that ministry is God's work. The Corinthian church is the result of God's activity ('you are God's field, God's building', v. 9) and Paul and Apollos are simply part of the process that God used to bring this about. God is at work and he calls them to be partners with him in accomplishing his plans. It is a collaboration, and they are not working for God but with God. The more conscientious we are, the more we are likely to take the responsibility for the outcomes of ministry on our own shoulders, but, properly understood, the responsibility lies with God as it is his work. Yes, we must do our very best, but, ultimately, it is God's work and we must leave the results with him.

Prayer
Lord, help me to rest in you.

Tony Horsfall

Equipping others

You then, my son, be strong in the grace that is in Christ Jesus. And the things you have heard me say in the presence of many witnesses entrust to reliable people who will also be qualified to teach others. Endure hardship with us like a good soldier of Christ Jesus.

My formative years in Christian ministry took place in cross-cultural mission, leading a newly formed church that was part of a national denomination in East Malaysia. Our strategy was simple: to raise up other leaders as quickly as possible, working ourselves out of a job, so that the indigenous church could stand on its own two feet.

Paul's philosophy of ministry as described here was the inspiration for this approach and the conviction that ministry is about equipping others has stayed with me ever since. It is, I believe, the most effective way of building strong, healthy churches.

Paul had a close mentoring relationship with Timothy—like a father and son. From the moment that Paul invited the young man to join him on his travels (Acts 16:1–5) and become a sort of 'apprentice', he taught him the Christian faith and trained him in how to serve God. Now Timothy has been sent to help the church in Ephesus and Paul is writing to encourage his protégé and share further wisdom with him.

Notice that Paul's instruction to Timothy is to repeat this mentoring process with other reliable people, who will then do the same with others. Thus, a process of spiritual multiplication will take place and leaders will be raised up for the church in Ephesus who will be well-grounded in the faith and adequately equipped to serve God also.

The apostle appears to have strongly advocated that ministry is not so much about doing things for people as equipping people to do the work of ministry themselves. Thus, he writes about the ascended Christ: 'It was he who gave some to be apostles, some to be prophets, some to be evangelists, and some to be pastors and teachers, to prepare God's people for works of service, so that the body of Christ might be built up' (Ephesians 4:11–12).

Prayer

Lord, help me to invest my life in others.

Tony Horsfall

Words of advice

Don't let anyone look down on you because you are young, but set an example for the believers in speech, in conduct, in love, in faith and in purity. Until I come, devote yourself to the public reading of Scripture, to preaching and to teaching... Be diligent in these matters; give yourself wholly to them, so that everyone may see your progress. Watch your life and doctrine closely.

Two things stand out as we read these words of apostolic advice. The first is the importance of personal example in ministry. Whether we realise it or not (and whether we like it or not), people observe those in ministry and inevitably are influenced in their own behaviour by what they see. We should not be surprised by this. The best teaching is not just about imparting knowledge or passing on information. It is about modelling the things we are trying to communicate for those we teach. This is why Paul urges Timothy to watch his life and doctrine closely, for there must be a consistency between our words and our behaviour. The five areas itemised by Paul—speech, conduct, love, faith and purity —represent some of the most challenging areas of personal discipleship for us all, reminding us that only with God's help can any of us live with integrity.

The second thing to notice is the emphasis on growth and progress—what is termed nowadays 'personal development'. No one in ministry has 'arrived'; we are all a work in progress and on a continuing journey ourselves. Therefore, we should be continually seeking to know God more deeply, to allow the Spirit to bring healing and wholeness to our lives and develop and enhance the gifts Christ has given us. We should never reach the point where we feel satisfied or complete—a 'holy dissatisfaction' is a healthy motivation and keeps us pressing on.

The desire to provide a good example and the appetite to keep on growing both require a high degree of application and personal discipline. The call to ministry is not to be taken lightly. It demands the very best of us.

Prayer

Lord, give us grace to reflect you in every way.

Tony Horsfall

Staying the distance

> For I am already being poured out like a drink offering, and the
> time has come for my departure. I have fought the good fight, I
> have finished the race, I have kept the faith. Now there is in store
> for me the crown of righteousness, which the Lord, the righteous
> Judge, will award to me on that day—and not only to me, but also
> to all who have longed for his appearing.

Writing to Timothy, Paul is conscious that he may not have much time
left, so is in reflective mood. He sums up his ministry with three telling
images, each of which aptly describes Christian life and ministry.

'I have fought the good fight' (v. 7). There is no doubt that Paul
considered he was involved in a spiritual battle and this military metaphor provides an accurate description of the intense conflict in which
he often engaged with Satan and the powers of darkness (Ephesians
6:10–18; 2 Timothy 2:3–4). We should not expect ministry to be easy.
At times we will need to exhibit the same courage and strength of character as soldiers do in battle.

'I have finished the race' (2 Timothy 4:6). Paul would have been
familiar with the Corinthian games and aware of the discipline and
dedication that marked out the best athletes. He considered these qualities essential in Christian living and often likened his ministry to the
running of a long-distance race (1 Corinthians 9:24–27; 2 Timothy
2:5). It is not starting out that is important, but finishing well.

'I have kept the faith' (4:7). The apostle was aware that the gospel had
been entrusted to him like a precious possession and his responsibility
was to guard it safely. He had been faithful, like a good steward, in dis-
charging this responsibility, even when it meant hardship and persecu-
tion (1 Corinthians 4:1–2; 2 Timothy 1:14). Anyone called to ministry
must recognise the need to persevere and hold fast to the truth.

With the end in sight, then, Paul is not sad but expectant. He is
looking to the future, to the return of Christ and the rewards that those
who have served him well will receive.

Prayer

Lord, help me to finish well.

Tony Horsfall

Hezekiah: goodness under pressure

It is 701BC. The situation is stark. Nearly 20 years earlier, Israel, the northern kingdom, had succumbed to the brutal Assyrian invaders, God's judgment on its sin. They had been warned, countless times. The message was clear: 'Worship the Lord your God; it is he who will deliver you from the hand of all your enemies' (2 Kings 17:39). Tragically, their disobedience was just as clear: 'They would not listen… They followed worthless idols and themselves became worthless' (vv. 14–15) so the Assyrians dragged them off into exile.

Assyria was awesomely powerful—the greatest empire thus far in world history. Peoples and nations were crushed, swept aside by its army that could call on 300,000 men and smash the enemy with its heavy chariots. Now that army was headed to Jerusalem to swat the rebellious but insignificant Judah, as one would an irritating bluebottle. They had the might, they had the strength: what could possibly go wrong?

Judah was ruled by Hezekiah. His name should have given the Assyrians food for thought as it means 'God is my strength'. Unlike most of the other kings of Israel and Judah at this time, Hezekiah was determined to live up to his name. He took God seriously. He set about reforming the religious worship of the people, destroying idols and shrines, purifying the temple. He threw off foreign domination, defeating the Philistines, just like his forefather David. Also like David, it was said that 'the Lord was with him', even though, like David, he was far from perfect. Now his goodness, his trust in God, was to face its sternest test. He must have felt a little like David had done when he went out on to the battlefield to face Goliath. That great external challenge was echoed in a very private challenge—his own health and mortality.

As we explore together the story of how Hezekiah coped with these challenges, you may be facing challenges of your own and you will know others who feel surrounded by an enemy or threatened by ill health. My prayer is that there may be some valuable insights from this story of ancient history—not least because the God who was Hezekiah's strength is the same God who can be our strength, by his Spirit.

Stephen Rand

2 KINGS 18:2–7 (NIV, ABRIDGED)

No one like him

[Hezekiah] reigned in Jerusalem for twenty-nine years... He did what was right in the eyes of the Lord, just as his father David had done... Hezekiah trusted in the Lord, the God of Israel. There was no one like him among all the kings of Judah, either before him or after him. He held fast to the Lord and did not stop following him; he kept the commands the Lord had given Moses. And the Lord was with him; he was successful in whatever he undertook. He rebelled against the king of Assyria and did not serve him.

What would you like to be written about you in the history books of the future? Hezekiah, in this history book, is given an outstanding endorsement as a king: 'There was no one like him' (v. 5). It is worth examining what made him qualify for this ultimate commendation and thinking how we might be marked on the same scorecard.

First, 'he did what was right' (v. 3). The standard for his behaviour was not set by his own assessment, but by God. It still is. We still have the 'commands the Lord had given Moses' (v. 6); our only aim should be to do what is right 'in the eyes of the Lord' (v. 3). Second, Hezekiah 'trusted in the Lord' (v. 5). When life was tough, he 'held fast' (v. 6); he would not let go of God—and God did not let go of him.

Third, he was brave enough to take risks and stand against the forces of evil that often threatened to dominate and overwhelm. He 'rebelled against the king of Assyria and did not serve him' (v. 7).

Hezekiah was king for 29 years. He had plenty of opportunity to make mistakes, but such was his consistency of character and behaviour that he is mentioned in the same breath as David and Moses. In Old Testament terms, it does not get better than that. The historian notes two results of Hezekiah living in God's world God's way: he knew God's presence ('the Lord was with him', v. 7) and he was successful.

Reflection

The only success worth having is that which is shaped by the presence and the word of God.

STEPHEN RAND

Paying the price

In the fourteenth year of King Hezekiah's reign, Sennacherib king of Assyria attacked all the fortified cities of Judah and captured them. So Hezekiah king of Judah sent this message to the king of Assyria at Lachish: 'I have done wrong. Withdraw from me, and I will pay whatever you demand of me.' The king of Assyria exacted from Hezekiah king of Judah three hundred talents of silver and thirty talents of gold. So Hezekiah gave him all the silver that was found in the temple of the Lord and in the treasuries of the royal palace.

Yesterday's glowing character reference is today a little tarnished. Faced with a terrifyingly powerful enemy, Hezekiah caves in. Completely. Abjectly. His rebellion had begun when he refused to pay tribute to the mighty Assyria. Now comes the reckoning, the 'tax collector' arriving in force to collect his arrears. 'The Assyrian came down like the wolf on the fold' was how Byron described it in his dramatic poem, 'The destruction of Sennacherib' in 1815. In one sentence (v. 13) the historian records the devastating impact of the invasion: all the fortified cities attacked; all the fortified cities captured.

The prophet Isaiah passed on God's urging that Hezekiah should not give way to fear (Isaiah 10:24), but trust God for victory. The plea fell on deaf ears. Hezekiah is prepared to do anything to avoid the fate of Israel. He apologises. He makes his confession, using words that would normally be addressed to God. He offers Sennacherib a blank cheque… and Sennacherib takes due delight in cashing it.

The result? Eleven tons of gold and silver are demanded, so Hezekiah is forced to strip the temple of its wealth. From now on, the focus of the worship of the people of God will show signs of the defeat. That which was precious and dedicated to God is wrenched off to feed a tyrant's greed. The cost is also personal. Contemporary records suggest that Sennacherib demanded at least two of Hezekiah's daughters for his harem. Sennacherib had his revenge. Hezekiah could not sink any lower.

Prayer

Gracious Father, loving Lord, grant all those who are faced with forces that seem all-powerful and are ready to overwhelm the strength to stand firm.

STEPHEN RAND

Who can be trusted?

The king of Assyria sent… a large army… to King Hezekiah at Jerusalem… The field commander said… 'Tell Hezekiah: "This is what the great king, the king of Assyria, says: on what are you basing this confidence of yours? You say you have the counsel and the might for war—but you speak only empty words. On whom are you depending, that you rebel against me?… But if you say to me, "We are depending on the Lord our God"—isn't he the one whose high places and altars Hezekiah removed, saying to Judah and Jerusalem, "You must worship before this altar in Jerusalem"?… The Lord himself told me to march against this country and destroy it."'

Hezekiah thought he had paid off Sennacherib, but the expense was for nothing. Sennacherib cannot be trusted: far from withdrawing, he sends an army against Jerusalem. Hezekiah's rebellion has clearly rankled with him. Hezekiah has failed to recognise just how great he—'the great king'—is; he imagines that he can trust someone else. Bullies much prefer it when their victims show their fear. Hezekiah did that when he paid up, of course, but this bully wants more.

Sennacherib is full of confidence. Israel had been crushed—and had they not trusted the same God? So, he sends his field commander with a message full of sneering mockery, apparently aiming to undermine Hezekiah in the eyes of his people. If you really are trusting God, Hezekiah is told, for all to hear, you have made two mistakes. First, you have just done away with a whole host of places where people could worship God. Second, your God has said that I am the agent of his judgment ('the rod of my anger', Isaiah 10:5).

This is psychological warfare, rooted in deception. It fits a biblical pattern that began in the garden of Eden—'Didn't God say… ?' Jesus faced it when confronted by the devil in the desert. Followers of Jesus are still tempted to abandon their trust in God by being shown a partial view of reality, backed up with a distortion of God's own words.

Prayer

Almighty God, loving Father, help me to trust you, however difficult the circumstances.

Stephen Rand

81

Choose life

Then the commander stood and called out in Hebrew, 'Hear the word of the great king... Do not let Hezekiah persuade you to trust in the Lord... Make peace with me and come out to me. Then each of you will eat fruit from your own vine and fig-tree and drink water from your own cistern, until I come and take you to a land like your own—a land of grain and new wine, a land of bread and vineyards, a land of olive trees and honey. Choose life and not death! Do not listen to Hezekiah, for he is misleading you when he says, "The Lord will deliver us." Has the god of any nation ever delivered his land from the hand of the king of Assyria?... How then can the Lord deliver Jerusalem from my hand?'

The attempt to undermine Hezekiah in the eyes of his people continues relentlessly. The king's negotiators try to get the Assyrian commander to speak in a language the people will not understand (v. 26). The commander twists the knife even further, emphasising that it is the people who will suffer if Hezekiah remains stubborn (v. 27).

He makes them an offer he is certain they will not be able to refuse: abandon Hezekiah (and God) for Assyria and look at the benefits—a new land, fruitfulness; life rather than death. The language echoes the promise God made to his people when they left Egypt for the 'promised land'. The temptation echoes the lie first told in Eden, revisited with Jesus in the wilderness and shouted from the rooftops in our own society: God's way is miserable, restrictive and mean; if you want the good things of life, turn your back on God.

Then comes the final, high-risk, overconfident taunt: 'Has the god of any nation ever delivered his land...?' This, though, is not one god among many; this is the God of the whole world, King of kings—and he will not be mocked.

Reflection

The greatest challenge for the church today is to demonstrate that the words from the hymn I sang when I was baptised are true: 'Trust and obey, for there's no other way to be happy in Jesus than to trust and obey.'

John H. Sammis (1887)

STEPHEN RAND

Facing disaster

When King Hezekiah heard this, he tore his clothes and put on sackcloth and went into the temple of the Lord. He sent Eliakim the palace administrator, Shebna the secretary and the leading priests, all wearing sackcloth, to the prophet Isaiah... They told him, 'This is what Hezekiah says: this day is a day of distress and rebuke and disgrace... It may be that the Lord your God will hear all the words of the field commander, whom his master, the king of Assyria, has sent to ridicule the living God, and that he will rebuke him for the words the Lord your God has heard. Therefore pray for the remnant that still survives.'

Sennacherib has overreached himself, offering what only God can provide: life in all its fullness. He is in a position of great strength, however, and Hezekiah in one of extreme weakness. So what can Hezekiah do?

First, he faces up to reality. He may be reacting to the desperate predicament of the nation or the insulting and blasphemous words reported to him. Either way, he is emotionally distraught, symbolised by the tearing of his clothes. He recognises that the pending disaster is a political and spiritual matter, by involving the national leaders of both government and religion, and he acknowledges his own helplessness.

Second, he turns to God in repentance (symbolised by putting on sackcloth). He knows that the only way he can come into God's presence, however great the crisis, is to adopt the attitude of the tax collector in Luke 18:13: 'God, have mercy on me, a sinner.'

Third, he looks for prophetic prayer from Isaiah. He admits that he needs all the help he can get, but he looks for that help from the spiritual resources God has given to him.

Finally, he holds on to what hope he can. Surely God will not allow his name to be belittled and his reputation sullied? He will have heard the proud insults of Sennacherib and will 'rebuke' the one responsible. Centuries later, Mary will rejoice because 'he has brought down rulers from their thrones' (Luke 1:52).

Reflection

How do I face up to potential disaster? Is there a pattern here to follow?

STEPHEN RAND

Do not be afraid

Isaiah said to them, 'Tell your master, "This is what the Lord says: do not be afraid of what you have heard—those words [that]... have blasphemed me. Listen! When he hears a certain report, I will make him want to return to his own country, and there I will have him cut down with the sword."'... Now Sennacherib received a report that Tirhakah, the king of Cush, was marching out to fight against him. So he again sent messengers to Hezekiah... 'Say to Hezekiah king of Judah: do not let the god you depend on deceive you when he says, "Jerusalem will not be given into the hands of the king of Assyria." Surely you have heard what the kings of Assyria have done to all the countries, destroying them completely.'

Isaiah replies to Hezekiah confidently: 'This is what the Lord says' (v. 6). God's prophet has the authority to speak out God's word (the problem was, God's people did not always recognise that authority).

The message starts, as do many of God's messages, with the words, 'Do not be afraid' (v. 6). Angels said it when they appeared to those chosen by God; Jesus said it to his disciples. It is more than a vaguely encouraging, 'Don't worry'; it is a command. When every human assessment of the situation suggests there is no hope, then this instruction seems perverse and unhelpful, but, of course, it is based on God's assessment. No situation is too difficult for him; nothing takes him by surprise. It is, then, entirely rational to look at God's love and power, rather than the immediate circumstance, and decide that there is no need to be afraid. The original Hebrew phrase carries a hint of the meaning 'do not give this your worship'. We are told to fear God; if we do that, then we have nothing else to fear.

Isaiah predicted and promised that Sennacherib would be diverted by a report, a rumour—and so he was. Isaiah also predicted and promised that he would be 'cut down' in judgment for his blasphemy—and so he was, 20 years later. Judgment was not swift, but it was sure.

Prayer

Lord, grant me the faith to trust you, whatever my circumstances, so that I do not need to be afraid.

STEPHEN RAND

2 KINGS 19:14–19 (NIV, ABRIDGED)

Hezekiah's prayer

Hezekiah received the letter… Then he went up to the temple of the Lord and spread it out before the Lord. And Hezekiah prayed to the Lord: 'Lord, the God of Israel, enthroned between the cherubim, you alone are God over all the kingdoms of the earth… Give ear, Lord, and hear; open your eyes, Lord, and see; listen to the words Sennacherib has sent to ridicule the living God. It is true, Lord, that the Assyrian kings have laid waste these nations and their lands… Now, Lord our God, deliver us from his hand, so that all the kingdoms of the earth may know that you alone, Lord, are God.'

So far, the conversations have been through intermediaries. Hezekiah had asked Isaiah to pray and now he prays himself. He consciously enters the presence of God by going to the temple. Remember, like Hezekiah, we can talk directly to our Creator. We have no need of intermediaries, nor do we need to go to a special building or location. God lives in us by his Spirit; we are his temple. We can speak to him anywhere, anytime—and not just in an emergency. Why do we pass up this opportunity so often?

Hezekiah spreads out the letter before the Lord and invites God to respond. Notice how he constructs his prayer. He locates the God of Israel as being 'enthroned between the cherubim' (v. 15). This is probably a reference to the cherubim that were positioned on the top of the ark of the covenant in the Holy of Holies, their wings stretched out over the mercy seat. The significance of the phrase is perhaps clearer than its precise meaning. Most ancient peoples thought of their gods as distant, but the God of Israel made his home at the centre of his people, in the heart of the nation. Then Hezekiah affirms the exact opposite of Sennacherib's view: the God of Israel is the only true God, 'over all the kingdoms of the earth' (v. 15), including Assyria. The focus of his prayer is not so much the deliverance of the people as the vindication of God himself. Hezekiah wants the truth about God to be revealed and Sennacherib's slurs silenced.

Reflection

Whose reputation do we care about most? Our own—or God's?

STEPHEN RAND

2 KINGS 19:20–22, 28 (NIV, ABRIDGED)

Judgment promised

Then Isaiah… sent a message to Hezekiah: 'This is what the Lord, the God of Israel, says: I have heard your prayer concerning Sennacherib king of Assyria. This is the word that the Lord has spoken against him: "… Who is it you have ridiculed and blasphemed? Against whom have you raised your voice and lifted your eyes in pride? Against the Holy One of Israel!… Because you rage against me and because your insolence has reached my ears, I will put my hook in your nose and my bit in your mouth, and I will make you return by the way you came."'

God is not mocked. Hezekiah has prayed that God will vindicate his reputation, so publicly rubbished by Sennacherib. Isaiah sends him a message, part one of which reveals what God has said to Sennacherib. Hezekiah is reassured that the world will see the Assyrian king humbled by 'the Holy One of Israel' (v. 22).

The Assyrian exhibits in the British Museum are most impressive. There are massive sculptures, a stunning reconstruction of imposing city gates, an obelisk decorated with images of an earlier Assyrian king receiving tribute from Israel, and many reliefs depicting episodes from Assyrian history. This is how we know that when Assyrians took captives in battle, they led them in triumph with a hook in their nose.

The message is stark and simple. Those who set up their power and might against God will discover that God is the Almighty God. All others rule by God's providence and permission. Sennacherib's pride was directly focused on God. He deliberately insulted and mocked him as he was convinced his behaviour carried no risk.

All sin is rebellion against God. Our own pride is a denial of our dependence on God and, as a result, we are all subject to God's judgment. The good news is that, if we acknowledge our own weakness and pride, we can find mercy through Christ. Sennacherib discovered that his pride would cause him to get his just deserts. Praise God that he has made it possible for us to choose life, life with God himself.

Prayer

Lord, we give you humble thanks for your love, your grace and mercy.

STEPHEN RAND

The promise

'This will be the sign for you, Hezekiah: This year you will eat what grows by itself, and the second year what springs from that. But in the third year sow and reap, plant vineyards and eat their fruit. Once more a remnant of the kingdom of Judah will take root below and bear fruit above. For out of Jerusalem will come a remnant, and out of Mount Zion a band of survivors. The zeal of the Lord Almighty will accomplish this.'

Isaiah's message from God, part two, is one of hope for Hezekiah. The aftermath of the Assyrian assault would not be easy, but there would be food: two years of wild plant food, then normal farming could take over. This provision of food from the land, despite the ravages of the Assyrian army, was a sign that God was not going to abandon his people. Rather, there would be a remnant, a band of survivors.

So often in history the situation for God's people has looked hopeless, but God does not abandon them: he has promised to be with them. Sometimes the hope and the future are hanging by a thread, but it is still there, ready to burst into fullness of life.

Last summer, we replanted our small garden. Then winter came and it was cold right into the spring months. The passion flower that had done so well looked finished, lifeless. Today, though, I have noticed a handful of green shoots. It has survived! That it is a passion flower is appropriate because God is full of passion for seeing his promise of hope and redemption through to completion. 'The zeal of the Lord Almighty will accomplish this' is the same phrase used when promising the birth of a child who will be the Prince of Peace (Isaiah 9:6–7). Interestingly, the Hebrew word translated as 'zeal' is also used for jealousy in the context of marriage, but then God describes his relationship with his people as being like a marriage. His 'zeal', his passion, is focused on making it possible for people to be in relationship with him.

Prayer

Sustenance, fruitfulness, relationship—Lord, help me to be so rooted in you that I never lose hold on all that you provide.

STEPHEN RAND

I will defend this city

'Therefore this is what the Lord says concerning the king of Assyria: "He will not enter this city or shoot an arrow here. He will not come before it with shield or build a siege ramp against it. By the way that he came he will return; he will not enter this city, declares the Lord. I will defend this city and save it, for my sake and for the sake of David my servant."'

Isaiah's message from God part three is a direct answer to Hezekiah's prayer for deliverance—and a direct answer to Sennacherib's mocking question, 'How then can the Lord deliver Jerusalem from my hand?' (18:35). If you want to be pedantic, these verses do not describe how the deliverance will be achieved. Rather, they simply state that it will be absolute and complete, and not a shot will be fired: the battle will be won even before it begins. That is how great God is, even when faced with the most powerful human being and his army.

Hezekiah's prayer is answered positively, but not because of Hezekiah himself or his goodness. Jerusalem will be saved, first, 'for my sake' (19:34). Sennacherib had mocked God's power and doubted his word; Hezekiah had asked that the whole world should know that God is the King of kings and the Lord of lords. God can—and will—defend his good name.

Jerusalem will be saved, second, 'for the sake of David' (v. 34). This is more puzzling. Why should God be concerned about David, so long after his death? The answer is that God had promised David he would establish his throne for ever (2 Samuel 7:16). God had made that promise as a result of his relationship with David, and God keeps his promises.

So, Hezekiah had prayed—but he had not earned the reprieve himself. It was not down to him; it was entirely down to God. God's mercy was the result of God's grace.

Reflection

We have the promise of God's deliverance… and it is entirely based on what God has done for us in Jesus: it is 'by grace you have been saved, through faith… it is the gift of God' (Ephesians 2:8).

STEPHEN RAND

Judgment delivered

That night the angel of the Lord went out and put to death a hundred and eighty-five thousand in the Assyrian camp. When the people got up the next morning—there were all the dead bodies! So Sennacherib king of Assyria broke camp and withdrew. He returned to Nineveh and stayed there. One day, while he was worshipping in the temple of his god Nisrok, his sons Adrammelek and Sharezer killed him with the sword, and they escaped to the land of Ararat. And Esarhaddon his son succeeded him as king.

The judgment of God here is terrible and brutal. Sennacherib had sent his messengers to mock God; God sends his messenger (the meaning of the word 'angel') and the battle is over. They may have died from a virulent illness—disease was often attributed to 'the hand of God'—but whatever form it took, it was divine intervention. Some have suggested that the translation should be 185 officers rather than 185,000 soldiers. Either way, they were fighting for a king who had taken on the wrong enemy. They were not cut down by swords in a daytime battle; they were taken by surprise in the night. Jerusalem was delivered, as promised.

Sennacherib returned to his capital city. He fought another five military campaigns, but he never again took on Judah and Jerusalem. Some 20 years later he met his own judgment. The biblical historian cannot resist giving us the detail that he was murdered as he was 'worshipping in the temple of his god' (v. 37). His god proved unable to deliver him, unlike the God of Israel, who had delivered Jerusalem.

Sennacherib was granted 20 years of grace before God's day of justice arrived. We, too, live in what some have described as a 'day of grace'. The apostle Peter wrote, 'The Lord is not slow in keeping his promise, as some understand slowness. Instead he is patient with you, not wanting anyone to perish, but everyone to come to repentance. But the day of the Lord will come' (2 Peter 3:9–10).

Reflection

'If God is for us, who can be against us?' (Romans 8:31). Who—or what—are the tyrants that we need to stand against, so that they retreat to cause trouble no more?

STEPHEN RAND

2 KINGS 20:1–6 (NIV, ABRIDGED)

A second chance

In those days Hezekiah became ill and was at the point of death. The prophet Isaiah... went to him and said, 'This is what the Lord says: put your house in order, because you are going to die; you will not recover.' Hezekiah turned his face to the wall and prayed to the Lord, 'Remember, Lord, how I have walked before you faithfully and with wholehearted devotion and have done what is good in your eyes.' And Hezekiah wept bitterly. Before Isaiah had left the middle court, the word of the Lord came to him: 'Go back and tell Hezekiah... "... I have heard your prayer and seen your tears; I will heal you... I will add fifteen years to your life... I will defend this city for my sake and for the sake of my servant David."'

What a curious story! It seems to have happened when Hezekiah was under threat from Sennacherib. Perhaps it was a stress-related illness. Whatever its identity, Hezekiah was at the point of death; but then verse 7 reads, 'Isaiah said, "Prepare a poultice of figs." They did so and applied it to the boil, and he recovered.' A simple remedy or miraculous healing?

Hezekiah's reaction to being told his illness is terminal is perhaps also coloured by his state of mind. He 'turned his face to the wall' (v. 2) could also be translated as 'he sulked'!

I think we are all (especially men, just to be provocative!) prone to feeling that if we do God the favour of following him, then he should be good to us in return. So, of course, Hezekiah was right to pray. Reminding God what a good person he was, however, that he did not deserve this, was perhaps understandable but not revealing of great spiritual depth—more Pharisee than tax collector (Luke 18:10–14).

Books have been written on the topic 'Why do bad things happen to good people?' Part of the answer is that only one person was ever good enough to meet God's standards; the rest (including Hezekiah and me) are all sinners, reliant on God's mercy and grace. It is in his mercy and grace that God responds positively to Hezekiah's prayer!

Reflection

We may not always get our prayers right—but God always hears.

STEPHEN RAND

A sign

Hezekiah had asked Isaiah, 'What will be the sign that the Lord will heal me and that I will go up to the temple of the Lord on the third day from now?' Isaiah answered, 'This is the Lord's sign to you that the Lord will do what he has promised: shall the shadow go forward ten steps, or shall it go back ten steps?' 'It is a simple matter for the shadow to go forward ten steps,' said Hezekiah. 'Rather, let it go back ten steps.' Then the prophet Isaiah called on the Lord, and the Lord made the shadow go back the ten steps it had gone down on the stairway of Ahaz.

The story gets even more curious! My tentative conclusion is that Hezekiah was deeply depressed, a condition brought on by the stress of his situation. He has minor physical symptoms, but he feels like death. In his mind he is about to die—as Isaiah points out in a prophetically forthright way. So Hezekiah turns to God and is promised healing that comes from God's mercy, not earned by Hezekiah's goodness.

The promise is not enough, however: in his depressed state, he needs a sign. He asks, in effect, for the clock to be put back (the shadow on the steps is perhaps a reference to a giant ceremonial sundial). This miracle may also have helped him believe God regarding the greater miracle of the defeat of Sennacherib's army.

Whether or not my analysis is correct, it is still true that mental illness is a largely unacknowledged challenge to the church. God can heal the mind as he can heal the body, but insensitive interventions by well-meaning Christians are a risk, as is avoiding the issue.

Last year, the Archbishop of Canterbury's daughter, Katharine Welby, spoke of her depression, when she could see 'no hope in the world'. She said that she knows 'God will stand by me with every step', but it is a 'shame that so often his people will not'. She draws hope from the Bible, full of 'people who get miserable, angry, who hurt and who weep'.

Prayer

Lord, grant your church wisdom in responding to those with mental illness and give those who suffer a sign of your loving presence with them.

STEPHEN RAND

The bad and the ugly

Manasseh was twelve years old when he became king, and he reigned in Jerusalem for fifty-five years... He did evil in the eyes of the Lord... The Lord said through his servants the prophets: '... I will wipe out Jerusalem as one wipes out a dish, wiping it and turning it upside-down...' Amon was twenty-two years old when he became king, and he reigned in Jerusalem for two years... He followed completely the ways of his father... He forsook the Lord, the God of his ancestors, and did not walk in obedience to him. Amon's officials conspired against him and assassinated the king in his palace.

Hezekiah ruled for his further 15 years, but when he died, his example died with him. Manasseh opted for his grandfather's pattern of behaviour, rapidly undoing all the good Hezekiah had done.

The historian's account is utterly damning: what Manasseh did was just awful. He sacrificed his own son, burning him alive (v. 6), he rebuilt all the places of idol worship Hezekiah had destroyed (v. 3), he built altars to other gods in the temple (v. 5), he filled Jerusalem with the blood of the innocent and he led the people astray. The result was inevitable. The respite Hezekiah had won for the whole of Judah through his trust in God was wiped out by the torrent of evil unleashed by Manasseh, continued and reinforced by his son, Amon. Now God could only vindicate his name, his holiness, by executing judgment.

At 2 Kings 20 there is a record of the visit of a Babylonian delegation to Hezekiah. He showed them all his treasures: 'They saw everything in my palace' (v. 15). Isaiah then prophesies that all those treasures will be carried off to Babylon: 'Nothing will be left' (v. 16).

Hezekiah's response is revealing: '"The word of the Lord you have spoken is good," Hezekiah replied. For he thought, "Will there not be peace and security in my lifetime?"' (2 Kings 20:19). It seems that, having been granted a new lease of life, he rested. He failed to look ahead. Could he have done more to prepare his son for power? Leaders—and parents—carry a heavy burden.

Prayer

Lord, help me to invest in the future wisely in the power of your Spirit.

STEPHEN RAND

The Day of the Lord

The Day of the Lord refers not to one day, but a period of time. We use the word 'day' in the same way as when we say, 'this is the day of space travel' or 'this is the day of opportunity' or 'this is the day of...' —whatever'! The Day of the Lord is the whole period of time that marks God's intervention in the world until the end of history. Humankind has had its day and now it is God's time. The Day of the Lord includes Christ's return to earth (the second coming), testing (the tribulation), time of judgment, gathering together the living and the dead (the rapture) and reigning in glory (the millennium).

The Day of the Lord is one of the most-mentioned—but least-preached—topics in scripture. It is a subject at the heart of our Christian faith, but one that needs to be treated with humility. Any preacher who claims to know the time and place of Jesus' return is not being true to what the Bible says about the Day of the Lord. We do not know when or how it is going to take place (Mark 13:32) and we do not know what it will be like to meet face to face with the living God, 'For now we see only a reflection as in a mirror; then we shall see face to face. Now [we] know in part; then [we] shall know fully, even as [we are] fully known' (1 Corinthians 13:12).

The foundation of our faith is the life, death and resurrection of Jesus. The triumph of our faith is his ultimate victory over death. The headline news of the Christian faith is that this triumph over death happened for Jesus at his resurrection and will be evident for us all to see on the Day of the Lord (1 Thessalonians 4:16–17). Christ's ultimate victory over death gives us comfort when someone we love dies, courage to challenge injustice in society, determination to care for the poor, sick and vulnerable and urgency to tell others of the story of Christ's return. We will know when the day is here because, as lightning that comes from the east is visible even in the west, so will be the coming of the Son of Man (Matthew 24:27).

Bob Mayo

1 THESSALONIANS 5:1–2; 2 PETER 3:10; ACTS 2:20–21 (NIV)

Like a thief in the night

Now, brothers and sisters, about times and dates we do not need to write to you, for you know very well that the day of the Lord will come like a thief in the night... The heavens will disappear with a roar; the elements will be destroyed by fire, and the earth and everything done in it will be laid bare... 'The sun will be turned to darkness and the moon to blood before the coming of the great and glorious day of the Lord. And everyone who calls on the name of the Lord will be saved.'

The Day of the Lord is when Christ returns to earth. Jesus' first time on earth was as a carpenter's son and his return will be as a king. These are the two stages of the incarnation. The first stage culminated in Jesus' ascension to heaven. The second stage will come on the 'Day of the Lord' when Jesus personally and physically returns to earth. We will see the Son of Man (Jesus) sitting at the right hand of the Mighty One and coming 'on the clouds of heaven' (Matthew 24:30).

Knowing we live in in-between times and recognising that we cannot hurry Jesus' return, we learn to value patience and waiting as a part of our faith in Christ. Waiting for Christ to return is not simply a passive 'doing nothing'. Our waiting for Christ is more like the keen anticipation shown by the mother waiting at the school gate for her child to emerge. She cannot hurry the end of the school day and so she chats with some of the other parents, excited at the thought of seeing her child again.

In our society today, the idea of waiting for something is anathema—people want things immediately and on their own terms. We cannot hurry Jesus' return, though, and so, with the Holy Spirit sustaining us in our weakness (Romans 8:26) and fuelling our hope, we wait in anticipation of Christ's return in glory.

Reflection

Waiting is an expression of our faith in Christ and through this we learn to be patient with others and at peace with ourselves.

BOB MAYO

Now but not yet

So then, dear friends, since you are looking forward to this [the day of the Lord], make every effort to be found spotless, blameless and at peace with him. Bear in mind that our Lord's patience means salvation... Grow in the grace and knowledge of our Lord and Saviour Jesus Christ. To him be glory both now and for ever! Amen

The immediate significance of the Day of the Lord is not about judgment in the future, but living differently in the present. The important question for us is how our knowledge of its coming affects the way in which we live our lives here and now. The Day of the Lord is a key to the transformational, world-changing nature of the Christian faith. Our trust in the future coming of the Lord means that we are willing to put ourselves out for others and, if necessary, put up with difficult situations for the sake of a world in need of redemption. Jesus tells his disciples, 'blessed are those who mourn' because such people are suffering on behalf of the world (Matthew 5:4).

Our willingness to suffer for the sake of our future hope means that we are living as children of the light and the world is already being transformed daily by the love of Christ. This is referred to as 'realised eschatology'—*eschatos* being the New Testament Greek word for 'end', used with reference to the Day of the Lord and the end of the world. Realised eschatology signifies that the process of ending has already begun. The kingdom of heaven is 'now but not yet', 'here but still to come'.

In the Lord's Prayer, we say, 'Your kingdom come': it is a process in motion, still to come to completion. The kingdom of heaven is evident now in myriad different ways through the lives of Christian believers and will come in all its fullness on the final Day of the Lord. That coming day challenges all of us to live lives of purity and holiness.

Reflection

'And what does the Lord require of you? To act justly and to love mercy and to walk humbly with your God' (Micah 6:8).

BOB MAYO

No timetables

Concerning the coming of our Lord Jesus Christ and our being gathered to him, we ask you, brothers and sisters, not to become easily unsettled or alarmed by the teaching allegedly from us— whether by a prophecy or by word of mouth or by letter—asserting that the day of the Lord has already come.

There is such a thing as ignoring the possibility of the Day of the Lord coming, but there is also such a thing as being overprepared. The Thessalonians fell into this latter category because they were worried that Jesus might have already returned and they had actually missed him! There was a widespread belief that Jesus would return to earth during the lifetime of the first generation of believers—an idea that was in common currency even during Jesus' ministry. Martha had said to Jesus, 'I know he [Lazarus] will rise again in the resurrection at the last day' (John 11:24). When Jesus' disciples questioned him about the signs of the 'end of the age', he warned them that many would come in his name, claiming, 'I am the Messiah', and many would be taken in (Matthew 24:3–4), but he would be with them until the end of the age (28:20).

The context for our passage today seems to be that somebody was claiming that Paul or Silas or Timothy had received a prophetic revelation announcing that the time of the coming of Jesus was here. Perhaps there had been a letter from them to that effect. In these verses, Paul denies any such revelation or letter. What we learn from this is the importance of not letting our prayers be clouded by what we would like to happen, as the Thessalonians did. It is easy to let our prayers slip into different variations of asking for God's approval for what we want to do anyway. We cannot set timetables for God's sovereignty or work out when the Day of the Lord will be. Our responsibility is to pray in faith and wait in anticipation.

Reflection

The promise of the Day of the Lord makes it plain that God is sovereign over our lives and in control of history.

Bob Mayo

Prophecy fulfilled

'This is what was spoken by the prophet Joel: "In the last days, God says, I will pour out my Spirit on all people. Your sons and daughters will prophesy, your young men will see visions, your old men will dream dreams. Even on my servants, both men and women, I will pour out my Spirit in those days, and they will prophesy... The sun will be turned to darkness and the moon to blood before the coming of the great and glorious day of the Lord. And everyone who calls on the name of the Lord will be saved."'

At Pentecost, people were filled with the Holy Spirit and began to speak in other tongues as the Spirit enabled them (vv. 2–4). Peter tells the crowd that the coming of the Holy Spirit is the fulfilment of Joel's prophecy. The gathering of people and the outpouring of the Holy Spirit was the birth of the Church.

The Church represents a third period of history. The first period of history was that of the Old Testament. The second period was during the New Testament. The third phase of history is the time of the Church, which will lead up to the 'great and glorious day of the Lord' (v. 20). According to Peter, Joel's prophecy was fulfilled at Pentecost and so the time of the Church is the 'last days' to which Joel refers. From this we learn that the Day of the Lord is not some random event in history, disconnected from all that is happening now. It is the end of time for which the Holy Spirit is preparing us. Praying with the Holy Spirit is our preparation for the Day of the Lord. The Holy Spirit teaches us everything and reminds us of everything that Jesus has said (John 14:26). When we are weak, the Holy Spirit helps us; if we do not know what we ought to pray, the Spirit himself intercedes for us (Romans 8:26).

Reflection

Signs and wonders of the Holy Spirit, such as healing miracles in response to people's prayers, are a foretaste of what is still to come when God's fullness is revealed on the Day of the Lord.

BOB MAYO

Tribulation

People will be lovers of themselves, lovers of money, boastful, proud, abusive, disobedient to their parents, ungrateful, unholy, without love, unforgiving, slanderous, without self-control, brutal, not lovers of the good, treacherous, rash, conceited, lovers of pleasure rather than lovers of God.

The Day of the Lord will mean a time of trial and suffering (known as 'the tribulation') prior to the final judgment (Revelation 3:10). In the tribulation, we make our choice regarding God; in the hour of judgment, God makes his decision concerning us. Jesus refers to a time of great distress, unequalled from the beginning of the world until now and never to be equalled again (Matthew 24:21). It will be a time of God taking back control of the earth.

Any crisis brings to a head what is already in people's hearts and what is best and worst in human nature. Paul warns Timothy that he will see human nature at its very worst, as people are challenged by the burgeoning reality of Christ's return. This challenges us to recognise that the thoughts of our hearts contain the truth of who we are. The Day of the Lord challenges us to not be stressed (expecting nothing from people) or cynical (expecting the worst). The Day of the Lord urges us to face up to our real selves and accept that we do sometimes nurse grievances, take people for granted or end up proud and conceited. Our task is to recognise that salvation comes through Christ alone and put our trust in him.

Our trust in Christ is not simply a wager on eternity (as the French mathematician and philosopher Pascal described it) but a gesture of confidence in what is here and now. Our knowledge of the coming tribulation urges us to be at peace with others and face up to difficult situations in our lives.

Reflection

'God is faithful; he will not let you be tempted beyond what you can bear. But when you are tested, he will also provide a way out so that you can endure it' (1 Corinthians 10:13). 'For this God is our God for ever and ever; he will be our guide even to the end' (Psalm 48:14).

BOB MAYO

Together in God's presence

We will not all sleep, but we will all be changed—in a flash, in the twinkling of an eye, at the last trumpet. For the trumpet will sound, the dead will be raised imperishable, and we will be changed... Then the saying that is written will come true: 'Death has been swallowed up in victory.' 'Where, O death, is your victory? Where, O death, is your sting?' The sting of death is sin, and the power of sin is the law. But thanks be to God! He gives us the victory through our Lord Jesus Christ.

The pastoral logic of today's passage is that, on the Day of the Lord, we will meet again with those we have known before. This offers us comfort when someone close to us has died, although the gathering together of the living and the dead at the second coming does not mean that we live in exclusive marital relationships as we did before. We will all be together in God's presence and at the resurrection people will neither marry nor be given in marriage (Matthew 22:30).

The fact that the living and the dead will be drawn together on the Day of the Lord means that we can show courage at the funerals of those we love because we know their death is not the end of the story. Popular sentiment at funerals is often expressed in a poem written in 1932 by Mary Elizabeth Frye, 'Do not stand at my grave and weep', which says that we should not stand at a grave and cry, because the person is not there and did not really die. This sentiment is actually unrealistic and incorrect. Grief at someone's death and joy at Christ's return on the Day of the Lord go hand in hand. If we shy away from the reality of death, we deny ourselves the joy in Christ's victory over it. Mary Frye's poem suggests that people should seek consolation through signs of life in nature and see the person who has died in them—through wind, snow, sunlight or rain. These glimpses of life offer a temporary comfort to the bereaved, but the Day of the Lord offers a more substantial basis for hope.

Reflection

'Take heart!' said Jesus, 'I have overcome the world' (John 16:33).

BOB MAYO

Caught up

For the Lord himself will come down from heaven, with a loud command, with the voice of the archangel and with the trumpet call of God, and the dead in Christ will rise first. After that, we who are still alive and are left will be caught up together with them in the clouds to meet the Lord in the air. And so we will be with the Lord for ever. Therefore encourage one another with these words.

The point at which the living and the dead are caught up in the clouds to meet with Christ is what is commonly referred to as the 'rapture'. The English word 'rapture' is not in the Bible (but then neither is the word 'Bible' nor 'Trinity'!) The Latin translators of the Bible used the word *rapturo*—the root of the English word 'rapture'—to mean 'caught up', which is what this passage from Thessalonians says will happen to those of us who are still alive—we will be 'caught up' in the clouds to meet with our Lord.

It is striking that the Bible's ultimate vision of Christian hope is an image of crowds—and crowds of people gathered together. In our contemporary society, we often make a virtue of separation. It is an achievement if someone is able to buy their own home and a natural thing to give others 'space'. When we interpret the Day of the Lord through our own cultural lenses, we slip into the default position of assuming that it is simply about individual people being judged for their individual sins. We make the same mistake when we think about death as individual people getting into heaven or not.

The basis of our faith is that Christ has overcome the power of death. This victory will be shown in Christ returning to earth on the Day of the Lord.

Reflection

Our good news is not a disembodied heaven, which individual spirits float off to after death. Our good news is the kingdom of heaven (in the figure of the returning Christ) coming down to earth and gathering together the living and the dead in the 'rapture'.

Bob Mayo

REVELATION 21:1–4 (NIV, ABRIDGED)

Faith and hope

Then I saw 'a new heaven and a new earth', for the first heaven and the first earth had passed away, and there was no longer any sea. I saw the Holy City, the new Jerusalem, coming down out of heaven... And I heard a loud voice from the throne saying, 'Look! God's dwelling-place is now among the people, and he will dwell with them. They will be his people, and God himself will be with them and be their God. "He will wipe every tear from their eyes. There will be no more death" or mourning or crying or pain, for the old order of things has passed away.'

The foundation of our Christian faith is the life, death and resurrection of Jesus. The Day of the Lord is Christ's final victory over death and this will mean a new 'dwelling-place' for God among the people. As God had been to the man and the woman in the garden of Eden—not only Creator but also intimate friend—so he will be to all humanity on the Day of the Lord.

This future hope establishes Christianity as entirely forward-looking. The Day of the Lord enshrines faith as a central virtue of our Christian belief. Faith is not just an appendix to a set of doctrines but at the heart of our relationship with Christ. Faith is our guarantee from God regarding things that may at present be unclear and unknown (Romans 8:24–25). Without faith, life loses its meaning (Lamentations 3:18), while in death (certainly from an Old Testament perspective) there is no further hope (Isaiah 38:18). Hope is stronger than optimism because, while the former is based on the promise of God, the latter is based on feelings. Faith is more than a feeling or wishful thinking about the future; it is more than experience or good fortune. Faith is a command based on God's great promise: 'I am making everything new' (Revelation 21:5).

Reflection
What difference does it make to you to think of faith as a command?

BOB MAYO

MARK 13:32–35 (NIV, ABRIDGED)

God only knows

'But about that day or hour [of the Lord] no one knows, not even the angels in heaven, nor the Son, but only the Father. Be on guard! Be alert! You do not know when that time will come. It's like a man going away: he leaves his house and puts his servants in charge... and tells the one at the door to keep watch. Therefore keep watch because you do not know when the owner of the house will come back.'

When the Day of the Lord comes, the world as we know it will end and we do not know when that will be. In the words of Hamlet (Act 5, Scene 2, Line 216), 'If it be now, 'tis not to come; if it be not to come, it will be now; if it be not now, yet it will come. The readiness is all.' The Day of the Lord makes us realise that we are not in charge of our own destiny. Jesus tells how 'two people will be in one bed; one will be taken and the other left' (Luke 17:34).

We cannot decide when this day will be because we cannot control the future, so we achieve nothing by worrying. Whenever we go on a plane, we trust our lives to the pilot's skill and professionalism and the Day of the Lord challenges us to do the same with God. Once we are on the plane, we do not improve the pilot's flying by worrying that something might go wrong! What worry and faith have in common is a sense of what is possible in the future. Worrying assumes that something will go wrong and it will be up to us to deal with it, while faith involves putting our trust in God. Jesus told his followers to 'seek first his kingdom and... do not worry about tomorrow, for tomorrow will worry about itself' (Matthew 6:33–34).

Reflection

The origin of 'goodbye' is 'God be with you'. We say this to our friends, knowing that the Day of the Lord may have come before we see them again, but, in saying goodbye, we commit them to God's loving care.

BOB MAYO

Judgment and mercy

And I saw the dead, great and small, standing before the throne, and books were opened. Another book was opened, which is the book of life. The dead were judged according to what they had done as recorded in the books. The sea gave up the dead that were in it, and death and Hades gave up the dead that were in them, and each person was judged according to what they had done.

Here, John records the climax of God's judgment in the book of Revelation: we are to be judged by how we measure up to the word of God. This idea of judgment is the core of the Bible's teaching about the Day of the Lord. We need to be ready for judgment day (2 Corinthians 5:10). We will have to give account for every empty word we have spoken (John 12:48).

It is easy to feel uncomfortable with the idea of judgment because we are used to having things on our own terms and do not like the idea of someone telling us that we are wrong. In our contemporary society, people want their religion neat and nice, affirmative, promoting moral values and encouraging good living. We like to think of God as loving and all-forgiving rather than as a God of wrath and anger. The psalmist makes it clear, however, that God's judgment does not mean vindictiveness or punishment: 'The decrees [judgments] of the Lord are firm and all of them are righteous. They are more precious than gold, than much pure gold; they are sweeter than honey, than honey from the honeycomb' (Psalm 19:9–10).

This all helps to bring into sharp relief the nature of our responsibility for how we choose to live our lives. If we place our trust in God, then all will be well, because the promise of God's judgment is also the promise of his grace. If we feel uncomfortable in talking about God's 'fierce anger', we should ask ourselves if it is because we are unused to talking about God's infinite forgiveness.

Reflection

We live in a society in desperate need of forgiveness. We ourselves can end up spending our lives looking for God's approval, not realising that it was there all along.

BOB MAYO

Judgment and forgiveness

For the day of the Lord is near in the valley of decision. The sun and moon will be darkened, and the stars no longer shine. The Lord will roar from Zion and thunder from Jerusalem; the earth and the heavens will tremble. But the Lord will be a refuge for his people, a stronghold for the people of Israel. Then you will know that I, the Lord your God, dwell in Zion, my holy hill.

God is hardwired to be a God of justice, and judgment on the Day of the Lord will mean that he brings about justice in society. This is good news to victims, but a day of reckoning for the oppressors. Those who are uncomfortable with the idea of judgment tend to be those who are materially comfortable and do not see why their world should be threatened. Our identification with the crucified Christ means having solidarity with the poor and dispossessed. The messianic hope was never the hope of the victors and the rulers, but always the hope of the defeated and ground down. The way in which we behave towards those who are the weakest and most in need is taken as the way we relate to Christ and we are judged accordingly ('Whatever you did for one of the least of these brothers and sisters of mine, you did for me', Matthew 25:40). What we learn from this is to identify those who are the most vulnerable and treat them with dignity and respect.

Judgment on the Day of the Lord is best understood as a question of accountability rather than punishment. The fact that we will all appear before the judgment seat of Christ (2 Corinthians 5:10) shows us that actions have consequences and it is up to us to take responsibility for how we live our lives. At the same time, we should reflect that God's judgment can actually free us from having to think about ourselves constantly by encouraging us to put our trust in his grace and forgiveness. The greater our understanding of God's judgment, the more we are able to appreciate that grace and forgiveness.

Reflection

Caring for those who are weaker than us is the quickest way to stop feeling sorry for ourselves.

BOB MAYO

Wise and foolish

'At that time the kingdom of heaven will be like ten virgins who took their lamps and went out to meet the bridegroom. Five of them were foolish and five were wise. The foolish ones took their lamps but did not take any oil with them. The wise ones, however, took oil in jars along with their lamps... While [the foolish ones] were on their way to buy the oil, the bridegroom arrived. The virgins who were ready went in with him to the wedding banquet. And the door was shut.

In Jesus' parable, the wise virgins are not able to share their oil with the foolish virgins because otherwise both sets of lamps would go out (vv. 8–9). As the wise virgins were ready for when the bridegroom appeared, so our challenge is to be properly prepared for the coming of Jesus.

Being prepared for the Day of the Lord means making sure that we know Jesus as our Lord and Saviour, so that we are able to recognise him when he comes. Being prepared means reading scripture and praying so that we know what God wants us to do; it means living our lives to please God and encouraging one another regarding the Lord's return. We are to tell other people about Jesus' return, too—this is the mandate of evangelism. Jesus' great commission to his disciples is passed down from generation to generation and is no less relevant for us today as it was for his followers then: 'All authority in heaven and on earth has been given to me. Therefore go and make disciples of all nations, baptising them in the name of the Father and of the Son and of the Holy Spirit, and teaching them to obey everything I have commanded you. And surely I am with you always, to the very end of the age' (Matthew 28:19–20).

Reflection

We become the 'foolish virgins' when we live without the reality of God in our lives. We become the 'wise virgins' when we are faithful and loving, putting our trust in his forgiveness and sharing the good news of Christ.

Bob Mayo

Trouble and desolation

[Jesus said] 'So when you see standing in the holy place "the abomination that causes desolation," spoken of through the prophet Daniel… then let those who are in Judea flee to the mountains. Let no one on the housetop go down to take anything out of the house. Let no one in the field go back to get their cloak. How dreadful it will be in those days for pregnant women and nursing mothers! Pray that your flight will not take place in winter or on the Sabbath. For then there will be great distress, unequalled from the beginning of the world until now—and never to be equalled again.'

Jesus quotes from Daniel (9:27), which describes an event in 167BC when a Greek ruler, Antiochus Epiphanes, set up an altar to Zeus in the temple in Jerusalem and on it sacrificed a pig. This event became known as the 'abomination of desolation'. Jesus warns those who are listening that a similar thing will happen in the future. What he prophesied took place in AD70 when the Roman armies surrounded Jerusalem and sacked the city. The passage is seen also as a reference to the difficult days that will precede the Day of the Lord.

This poses the perennial question of why bad things happen to good people. Why did the Romans sack Jerusalem with innocent people in the city? Why do some people have such difficult lives? It is an important question for us because, in our contemporary society (with endless consumption and choice on offer), we are tempted constantly to compare ourselves to others and decide whether they or we have the better life. On this basis, it is easy to feel hard done by or that life is unfair. On the Day of the Lord, we will realise that we are all alike in front of God and our jealousies and petty grievances will fall away before God's judgment throne. According to C.S. Lewis, if you took all the bad in the world and rolled it up into a single experience, then put it on a scale with the smallest moment of joy experienced by the least in heaven, it would not register any weight at all (*The Great Divorce*, 1945).

Reflection

Seek first his kingdom and his righteousness, and all these things will be given to you as well (Matthew 6:33).

BOB MAYO

In God's time

Christ has indeed been raised from the dead, the first fruits of those who have fallen asleep. For since death came through a man, the resurrection of the dead comes also through a man... The rest of the dead did not come to life until the thousand years were ended. This is the first resurrection... The sea gave up the dead that were in it, and death and Hades gave up the dead that were in them, and each person was judged according to what they had done.

The thousand years referred to in the first of our Revelation passages are known as the millennium. Some people take the thousand years figuratively and others take them literally. Some (pre-millenialists) believe that the millennium occurs before and others (post-millenialists) after Christ's second coming.

If we believe that the second coming happens before the millennium, then we believe that the millennium covers the whole great time block from the rapture (the gathering of the living and the dead) to the end of the kingdom of this world, which includes Armageddon. According to Revelation 16:16, Armageddon is the site of a final battle between good and evil during the end times. It is variously interpreted as a literal or symbolic location and is also used in a generic sense to refer to any 'end of the world' scenario.

The challenge posed to us by the concepts of the millennium and Armageddon is to accept that God is in control of history. This overturns our understanding of time. We naturally want to have things happen on our own terms, but, under God's eternal plan, that will never be so. All 24 hours a day and 168 hours a week belong to God. The Day of the Lord is based on the nature of God, not on human predictions; it is based on God's promises that at the end of time he will intervene in history. All we can do is pray and let God worry about the details.

Reflection

Even when our problems seem huge, we can rest in the Lord, knowing that he will work everything out and what we understand now only in part we will one day know fully (1 Corinthians 13:12).

BOB MAYO

God's transfiguring and liberating grace

During the 1990s, I had the privilege of teaching theology at a theological college and at a university. I particularly enjoyed introducing the world of theology to those who had never encountered it before—it was like helping people set out on a new journey. Usually, I encouraged them to focus their attention on two things. First, the idea of reflecting theologically—that is, creating a three-way conversation between whatever issues they might be wrestling with (moral, social, political), the religious tradition (God, Bible, sacraments and so forth) and themselves (current situation, possible prejudices, personal experience). I prefer the idea of 'conversation' to 'dialogue' as conversations are broader and more varied than dialogue and are never ends in themselves. Generally people converse because they believe that conversation is preferable to conflict and the latter is what often happens when there is no conversation. People also converse in the hope of generating new and better options for the way forward. Theologising this idea of conversation means becoming inspired by the promise of God's kingdom and recognising the way in which Christians are called to transform the present into what God always intended.

Second, I wanted to help the students grasp that theology could be 'done' in a variety of ways. The empirical model, for instance, is one that bases reflection on people's own experiences of God and the wider religious tradition. Such experiences are gathered and analysed to produce a whole model of theologising based on the resulting data. Then there is the pastoral approach, where theological reflection is generally a response to particular pastoral situations or part of the church's ministry in varying contexts. I personally prefer the liberation model, based on the biblical witness that God wants to set his people free. It involves the application of biblical insights and Christian traditions to real-life situations and provides doctrinal backing for those who seek a different and fairer world—a transfigured world.

During the next two weeks, I want to develop a conversation between this liberationist approach to doing theology and the needs of the world—a conversation that could well lead to a more transfigured way of living.

Andrew Jones

Witnessing oppression, not ignoring it

Then the Lord said, 'I have observed the misery of my people who are in Egypt; I have heard their cry on account of their taskmasters. Indeed, I know their sufferings, and I have come down to deliver them from the Egyptians, and to bring them up out of that land to a good and broad land, a land flowing with milk and honey, to the country of the Canaanites, the Hittites, the Amorites, the Perizzites, the Hivites, and the Jebusites… So come, I will send you to Pharaoh to bring my people, the Israelites, out of Egypt.'

From an Old Testament perspective, the Exodus story provides the first point of entry for understanding where the liberationist approach to 'doing theology' stems from. The story of Moses hearing God's call to set his people free portrays a God who sought to liberate the oppressed through an act of both deliverance and also political human liberation. The Israelites were delivered from a state of political subjection and, through their release, they eventually became a nation in their own right, a political entity. This act of liberation is all of a piece with the whole of God's activity throughout history because the original act of creation was itself an act of deliverance—a deliverance from chaos!

As mentioned in the introduction, those of us who take a liberationist approach insist that our theologising must begin with real-life situations in the real world. As Christians, we are called to be committed to action and prayer, even to the extent of taking sides with those who are oppressed themselves or those struggling to free the oppressed. The Exodus story convinces me that we cannot seek refuge from injustice and oppression in some indefinable spiritual world. Such dualistic thinking is not an option for God's children. It is precisely in the heart of the struggle for liberation that we find God because 'liberation'—setting people free—is God's work.

Reflection

The growth of the kingdom of God happens in history, not beyond it. By playing our role in liberating historical events, however small, we will be contributing to growing that kingdom. When Moses said 'yes' to God, that is what he recognised in him.

ANDREW JONES

Stepping forward again... this time fully

The true light, which enlightens everyone, was coming into the world. He was in the world, and the world came into being through him; yet the world did not know him. He came to what was his own, and his own people did not accept him. But to all who received him, who believed in his name, he gave power to become children of God, who were born, not of blood or of the will of the flesh or of the will of man, but of God. And the Word became flesh and lived among us, and we have seen his glory, the glory as of a father's only son, full of grace and truth.

Reading this powerful opening to John's Gospel, I am struck by the uncompromising statement that God himself, without ceasing to be God, came to share human life and not just in but as a particular man, at a particular time and in a particular place. The human life that Jesus lived and the death he died are believed to have been the human life and death of God himself. This, for me, is what is meant by the creed's statement that Jesus Christ was truly God as well as being truly man. Ultimately, what validates a liberationist approach for me is the conviction that God was in Jesus. This is where we discover the very heartbeat of our Christian faith.

From a Christian perspective, it is belief in the incarnation that provides the fundamental justification for insisting theological reflection must begin from where we are and from real-life situations within the life of this world and not the next. It is here that God has chosen to reveal himself—in the history of the real world. Here is the location of the final revelation—the incarnation in the man of flesh and blood, Jesus of Nazareth. History is the place of encounter between God and human beings and salvation comes to us within the boundaries of our history.

Reflection

Oppression cannot be allowed to coexist alongside a gospel that proclaims release to the captives in the new exodus that came through Jesus Christ.

ANDREW JONES

JOHN 17:1–5 (NRSV, ABRIDGED)

Beginnings and endings: we need both

> Jesus... looked up to heaven and said, 'Father, the hour has come; glorify your Son so that the Son may glorify you, since you have given him authority over all people, to give eternal life to all whom you have given him. And this is eternal life, that they may know you, the only true God, and Jesus Christ whom you have sent. I glorified you on earth by finishing the work that you gave me to do. So now, Father, glorify me in your own presence with the glory that I had in your presence before the world existed.'

I have always visualised the Christian faith as being held by two essential hinges: Christmas and Easter—or incarnation and resurrection. Both signify the reality of the kingdom inaugurated in and through Jesus Christ. Yesterday, we considered part of the proclamation of the incarnation in John's Gospel; today we look at part of Jesus' 'after dinner speech', where he declares how his death will glorify God.

It is not enough to think about imitating 'kingdom values'—such qualities as the compassion, love, tolerance and self-sacrifice of Jesus, essential as those are. We should be even more concerned with the gospel challenge to deepen our understanding of this foundational truth—that the kingdom of God came to us in and through the incarnation and resurrection. Christmas and Easter do not simply invite us to gaze at the manger or ponder the cross; they demand that we recognise that both events point us to a God who has opted to draw close to us at every level in this life.

A faith in Christ rooted in the liberating power of the incarnation—the beginning of the good news—must also be concerned with the glory of the cross and resurrection. We cannot have one without the other because the beginning and ending of Jesus' earthly life are two parts of a single Christian narrative. Reading both events together, we affirm that God in Christ subjected himself to human oppression and, as such, revealed his liberating love.

Reflection

Christ is God with us. No matter into what depths of suffering we may sink, God was there before us.

ANDREW JONES

Things make sense on the hilltop

Now about eight days after these sayings Jesus took with him Peter and John and James, and went up on the mountain to pray. And while he was praying, the appearance of his face changed, and his clothes became dazzling white. Suddenly they saw two men, Moses and Elijah, talking to him. They appeared in glory and were speaking of his departure, which he was about to accomplish at Jerusalem... Then from the cloud came a voice that said, 'This is my Son, my Chosen; listen to him!'

During the past few days I have mentioned several times how my way of engaging with theology is by relating it directly to real life—and how liberation theology is all about Christ giving his people the opportunity to be free. I also think it is useful to have a particular Bible narrative or story to form a 'backbone' to much of what we say or think theologically. When I was accompanying theological students on their new journey of training, I enjoyed encouraging them to search out a biblical narrative that they could use to shape their explorations.

For many years my own chosen narrative has been the story of Jesus' transfiguration and I have tried to make this story the 'backbone' of my personal journey of faith. A transfigured life is what follows from an authentic experience of God's liberation—from accepting his invitation to be 'set free'. At the same time, the truth is, I think, that the transfiguration of Jesus in some ways remains incomplete, until it is fully embraced as a way of life by Christians seeking to live out the good news today. One of the most profound insights I have come across to do with transfiguration is that when we look at the transfigured Christ, we ourselves can be transfigured and set free. Thus, we become the means by which others can start to share in this new way of living. That is liberation!

Reflection

Today, many churches celebrate the transfiguration of Christ as a feast day. Maybe we should be less concerned to talk about the transfiguration as an event on a mountain in Palestine and more about it in terms of an experience that is still freely available.

ANDREW JONES

MARK 9:9–13 (NRSV)

Keep quiet! There is more to come

As they were coming down the mountain, [Jesus] ordered them to tell no one about what they had seen, until after the Son of Man had risen from the dead. So they kept the matter to themselves, questioning what this rising from the dead could mean. Then they asked him, 'Why do the scribes say that Elijah must come first?' He said to them, 'Elijah is indeed coming first to restore all things. How then is it written about the Son of Man, that he is to go through many sufferings and be treated with contempt? But I tell you that Elijah has come, and they did to him whatever they pleased, as it is written about him.'

Although the Gospels vary regarding some of the detail of what happened at the top of that mountain of transfiguration, they agree about placing the event as a 'threshold' moment in Jesus' ministry. The 'penny dropped' for Peter, James and John at the top of that mountain, which became a sacred space for them, and they caught a glimpse of God's glory as it unfolded before their very eyes. For Mark (9:2–8) as for Matthew (17:1–13), the event happens between two predictions of Jesus' death, but for Mark, the experience is an anticipation of that final coming of God's kingdom. For him, the full significance of the transfiguration cannot be understood until after the resurrection.

Recently I was on retreat at a Franciscan friary where the conductor invited us to focus on our weaknesses in order to discover the reality of God's strength in new and invigorating ways. He described our 'inner places', those places where we go in order to ponder our weaknesses, as 'sacred spaces'. If we focus on our own weaknesses and vulnerabilities—while always in the light of the reality of God's strength—we can come to a place where we can 'own' those things and allow God to transfigure them, equipping us to move on freely on our journey.

Reflection

That glimpse of glory on the mountaintop prepared Jesus' friends,
in all their weakness and vulnerability, for what lay ahead
in their own life journey.

ANDREW JONES

Maybe... but tell me what you think

Now when Jesus came into the district of Caesarea Philippi, he asked his disciples, 'Who do people say that the Son of Man is?' And they said, 'Some say John the Baptist, but others Elijah, and still others Jeremiah or one of the prophets.' He said to them, 'But who do you say that I am?' Simon Peter answered, 'You are the Messiah, the Son of the living God.' And Jesus answered him, 'Blessed are you, Simon son of Jonah! For flesh and blood has not revealed this to you, but my Father in heaven.'

The evening before I was ordained, the bishop preached a sermon in which he gave a small group of us important 'tips' for life in ministry. One of them was, 'When you talk about God, tell the people about your experiences of him, not only what others have described in books.' Over the years I have valued that bit of advice.

In much the same way, Jesus asked his disciples who they thought he was—not necessarily wanting to know what others had told them. Interestingly, in the Gospel this question is sandwiched between two very important events concerning Jesus' true identity. On the one hand, the Pharisees ask for signs (16:1–4), revealing their spiritual blindness. On the other hand, the transfiguration (17:1–13) reveals liberation from such blindness. The passage we are looking at today, however, does not simply raise questions concerning the identity of Jesus; it goes further and leads to a commissioning. Once Jesus has been identified— once people know him and are able to tell others who he is—then there is work to be done (16:18–20).

Our ability to join in God's mission begins with our knowledge of him, but this always leads us on to work with him. The divide in the Gospels was not simply between those who recognised Jesus and those who did not, but, rather, between those who were prepared to follow him on the way of suffering and those who were not.

Reflection

Theologian Dietrich Bonhoeffer, hanged in 1945 for the part he played in a plot to kill Hitler, encouraged Christians to keep asking a question: not who Jesus 'was' then, but who Jesus 'is' for me today.

ANDREW JONES

Keep asking the reassuring questions

For ask now about former ages… ever since the day that God created human beings on the earth; ask from one end of heaven to the other: has anything so great as this ever happened or has its like ever been heard of? Has any people ever heard the voice of a god speaking out of a fire, as you have heard, and lived? Or has any god ever attempted to go and take a nation for himself from the midst of another nation, by trials, by signs and wonders, by war, by a mighty hand and an outstretched arm, and by terrifying displays of power, as the Lord your God did for you in Egypt before your very eyes?

Something about this passage reminds me of a creed, but, unlike traditional creeds still recited in churches today, this one occurs as a series of important questions. Nowadays, most scholars agree that the book of Deuteronomy reached its present shape possibly as late as the Babylonian exile in the sixth century BC, after a long process of formation. That was a time when the Israelites were encouraged to remember the great events of the past in order to preserve their traditions and do all they could to protect their historical identity. Indeed, believing in the great events of the past was precisely what gave them the hope and trust they so desperately needed during those difficult years of exile. Revisiting those events provided them with a sense of who they were, their high calling and unique vocation. Consequently, Deuteronomy links that unique vocation to the uniqueness of God. By asking these creed-like questions in the context of an oppressive exile, the Israelites sowed the seeds of hope that would eventually strengthen their return home and bring about their liberation.

Today, the Anglican Church remembers Mary Sumner, founder of the Mothers' Union in 1921. Recently, the Mothers' Union launched a campaign to 'sow seeds' in order to nurture faith and transform injustices. If we do not sow seeds, we cannot expect any kind of harvest.

Reflection

Growth and nurture in faith will pave the way for renewal and transformation—this is the stuff of liberation and transfiguration.

ANDREW JONES

Transfiguration... and then be free

Rejoice in the Lord always; again I will say, Rejoice. Let your gentleness be known to everyone. The Lord is near. Do not worry about anything, but in everything by prayer and supplication with thanksgiving let your requests be made known to God. And the peace of God, which surpasses all understanding, will guard your hearts and your minds in Christ Jesus.

My father was a photographer and I have only recently reflected that, on the whole, photographers must have happy lives because their services are generally called for on joyous occasions—weddings and celebrations! As the only photographer in a rural community, my father's Saturdays were usually taken up with weddings and, as a child, I would regularly accompany him to carry tripods, spare batteries and so on. I got to know not only the local churches and chapels but also the hotel kitchens, where I was fed while my father took the reception photos. I now remember something else: my father's usual words to the various wedding groups were, 'Stand still, smile and be yourself.'

In many ways, this threefold instruction sums up the essence of transfiguration and liberation. We must begin by 'standing still', so as to hear the voice of God, then smile, because his voice is one that moves us towards life. Finally, the voice says, 'You can be yourself—I am giving you permission to be yourself.'

Today, the church remembers Laurence, a deacon in Rome who was martyred in AD258. Traditionally, two things are known about him: he had the reputation of being attentive to God's voice and he was known for sharing God's voice in simple ways. One day, he was asked to deliver the treasures of the church to the Prefect of Rome. Instead, he distributed them among the poor and, in turn, presented the poor people to the Prefect, saying, 'Here is the treasure of the church.'

Reflection

The people—you and I—continue to be the true treasure of the church, but that treasure becomes more and more precious as we still ourselves and are attentive to God's word, so we can smile and truly hear God's permission for us to be ourselves.

ANDREW JONES

Come and do some work with me

Now the Lord said to Abram, 'Go from your country and your kindred and your father's house to the land that I will show you. I will make of you a great nation, and I will bless you, and make your name great, so that you will be a blessing. I will bless those who bless you, and the one who curses you I will curse; and in you all the families of the earth shall be blessed.' So Abram went, as the Lord had told him; and Lot went with him. Abram was seventy-five years old when he departed from Haran.

One of the themes running through the Old Testament is the Israelites' concern with their relationship as a nation with both God and the world in which they lived. They recognised that, as a people, their journey began in 'clay' (Genesis 2) and so, while life was essentially mortal and vulnerable, it also suddenly began to flourish when God vitalised the 'clay' and gave it spirit. This spirit or 'breath of God' is the overwhelming Old Testament principle of life. Through it human beings have been gifted with a godly dignity that becomes an integral part of the divine–human relationship.

In the passage today, we see the basis of that unique relationship between God and humanity—the covenant. Although the idea of a covenant is used in various ways throughout the Old Testament, it is the one between God and human beings that emerges as dominant. One of the most important of all such covenants was between God and Abraham. He not only conversed with God and encountered him as no one else did but he was also among the very first people to ever say 'yes' to God—and that 'yes' was crucial. What happened between God and Abraham is a reminder of how faith is rooted in the initiative that God takes to establish a deep and lasting relationship with us. It is then up to us to say 'yes'.

Reflection

Through the covenant, God breathes into us the breath of life and we become truly living beings, gifted with his dignity. The sharing of this dignity enables liberation to take place in our lives—and the lives of others.

ANDREW JONES

Keep it personal

The days are surely coming, says the Lord, when I will make a new covenant with the house of Israel and the house of Judah. It will not be like the covenant that I made with their ancestors when I took them by the hand to bring them out of the land of Egypt—a covenant that they broke, though I was their husband, says the Lord. But this is the covenant that I will make with the house of Israel after those days, says the Lord: I will put my law within them, and I will write it on their hearts; and I will be their God, and they shall be my people.

At the time when the prophets occupied centre stage and their ministry provided an effective pastoral role, talk of a covenant was not as prominent as it had been in the first five books of the Old Testament. What is striking, however, is that the experience of a covenant is woven through the entire prophetic message, more often than not without actually mentioning the word. Prophets such as Amos, Hosea, Isaiah and Micah, throughout their ministry, present the people with the true meaning of what it meant to be in a covenant with God. In other words, what it meant to live under his sovereignty and also his transfiguring acts of liberation and love.

Something different occurs in Jeremiah's ministry, however, offering a new perspective on this covenant relationship. In his challenge to the people he shows that it is precisely because the covenant is both a source of obligation and a blessing that God is faithful to his covenanted people, even when they are punished for their violations. Here, Jeremiah imagines the future of Israel in terms of a brand new covenant. He stresses that it is all about finding ways to establish a personal relationship with God, not so much a formal one between God and the whole nation. That was quite a shift.

Reflection

Just as in the new covenant called for by Jeremiah, where the individual is invited to say a very personal 'yes' to God, may our 'yes' be from the heart—and not only in word but in action too.

ANDREW JONES

Topsy-turvy thinking

The disciples came to Jesus and asked, 'Who is the greatest in the kingdom of heaven?' He called a child, whom he put among them, and said, 'Truly I tell you, unless you change and become like children, you will never enter the kingdom of heaven. Whoever becomes humble like this child is the greatest in the kingdom of heaven. Whoever welcomes one such child in my name welcomes me.'

Nowadays, depending on our church tradition, we may seek moral guidance primarily from scripture, authoritative rulings, church leaders or elsewhere. The underlying assumption is that a comprehensive set of principles is available to provide, always and everywhere, reliable guidance on how we should conduct our lives. Where do these universal principles come from and do they really help us make moral decisions?

I could have chosen one of many stories showing Jesus' topsy-turvy way of thinking about how best to live a moral life. Almost all his ethical standpoints were—and continue to be, today—completely counter-cultural. What principle, for instance, drove Jesus to reject out of hand the anxious concern of his mother and other family members and friends who sought to 'save' him from himself (Mark 3:20–21)? Again and again, we see Jesus making choices that have nothing to do with the religious rules and principles of the day. What we see instead is the possibility of conversion into a many-splendoured and more ambiguous reality than the seemingly tidy and secure world of rules and universal principles. This is what 'counter-cultural' really means.

Dietrich Bonhoeffer, in his book *Ethics*, writes about his involvement in the plot to overthrow Hitler and argues against speaking about this in terms of right and wrong. That would, he says, concede too much to the world of rules and principles. For Bonhoeffer, morality starts with unlearning the knowledge of good and evil as the world understands it. Instead, morality must begin with seeking a liberated and transfigured life for all—not just the holy huddle.

Prayer

Please, Lord, let me follow your example and put the person before the principle, even if it means being topsy-turvy.

ANDREW JONES

JOHN 15:12–17 (NRSV, ABRIDGED)

Expectations and privilege

'This is my commandment, that you love one another as I have loved you. No one has greater love than this, to lay down one's life for one's friends. You are my friends if you do what I command you. I do not call you servants any longer... but I have called you friends, because I have made known to you everything that I have heard from my Father. You did not choose me but I chose you. And I appointed you to go and bear fruit, fruit that will last, so that the Father will give you whatever you ask him in my name. I am giving you these commands so that you may love one another.'

Near where I live is a large Polish community and I have made many friends among its members over the years, including a Franciscan friar with whom I have visited Poland on a number of occasions. During my first visit, when we were travelling from Warsaw to Krakow, we stopped for lunch at a Franciscan convent in Oswiecim. Here is to be found one of the most distressing and shocking sites in Europe—Auschwitz—and that afternoon, the friar, accompanied by one of the sisters, took me there. On arrival, they headed straight to the cell of a man called Maximilian Kolbe, who had died there.

That day, I realised that Auschwitz was not only a place of horror but also a place of martyrdom. In the summer of 1941, the Nazis chose ten men at the camp to die in a starvation bunker as a reprisal for an escape. Kolbe, who was a Franciscan Catholic priest, asked to take the place of one of the condemned, a married man with a family. It was recorded that Kolbe not only died with the others but also helped them to die as gently as possible. He led them in prayer and praises, thus briefly converting that underground bunker of death into a place of liberation and transfiguration.

Reflection

On this day, the church commemorates Kolbe. We give thanks for his courage and commitment, which gave him the power to confront his captors with the love they sought to destroy. Here was a man who witnessed to a liberating and transfiguring God.

ANDREW JONES

The bearer of the incarnation

The angel Gabriel was sent by God to a town in Galilee called Nazareth, to a virgin engaged to a man whose name was Joseph... The virgin's name was Mary... The angel said to her, 'Do not be afraid, Mary, for you have found favour with God. And now, you will conceive in your womb and bear a son, and you will name him Jesus. He will be great, and will be called the Son of the Most High... Then Mary said, 'Here am I, the servant of the Lord; let it be with me according to your word.'

Today, many churches celebrate the assumption of Mary. The story of her life shows her to be a woman who was transformed and ultimately transfigured. On at least two occasions, though, she may have struggled to understand God's will—something that should encourage all of us who struggle to understand God's work in our lives. Mary was caught up in turmoil when the angel told her about her strange and unexpected pregnancy and, again, at the foot of the cross, as she gazed into the eyes of her dying son.

We usually tell the story of the annunciation in the light of Mary's response, but I like to think of it in terms of God's coming, in the person of Gabriel, to announce his love for Mary or, rather, for the people whom Mary represents. These people had an on/off relationship with God for so long, but now God tells them, you are ready, in the person of Mary, to receive the greatest gift of all and attain the salvation for which you long. That salvation is achieved in the passion of Christ and the cross—and Mary is there, too.

We see the grace of transfiguration in Mary as she comes through these times of perplexity. At the annunciation, grace is revealed as she sings her hymn of exultation (Luke 1:46–55) and, at the cross, as Jesus gives her into John's care (John 19:26–27)—precious moments indeed.

Prayer

Lord, thank you for this great gift of love and for your grace constantly at work in us. Help us to imitate and follow Mary's example of complete trust in you.

ANDREW JONES

Keep saying 'yes' to God

For the Son of God, Jesus Christ, whom we proclaimed among you, Silvanus and Timothy and I, was not 'Yes and No'; but in him it is always 'Yes'. For in him every one of God's promises is a 'Yes'. For this reason it is through him that we say the 'Amen', to the glory of God. But it is God who establishes us with you in Christ and has anointed us, by putting his seal on us and giving us his Spirit in our hearts as a first instalment.

New Testament writers clearly believed that, in Christ, all the promises of God recorded in scripture were fulfilled (2 Corinthians 1:20). When Paul describes his conversion to Agrippa, he says that the Lord was sending him to the Gentiles 'to open their eyes so that they may turn from darkness to light' (Acts 26:18). The opening of the eyes of the blind is a prominent theme in the prophecies of Isaiah, so Paul here sees himself as fulfilling Old Testament prophecy through his activity as an apostle. By implication, Christ continues to work through his church to bring the promises of the Old Testament even closer to fulfilment. Some of these promises are very much concerned with political and social justice, with liberating the oppressed and establishing peace between nations. Perhaps, then, liberation theology has got it right: the fulfilment of these ancient promises should be achieved through the involvement of the contemporary church in movements for political and social justice.

When all is said and done, however, as Christians, we have to read the Old Testament in the light of the New. Certainly, there is much we can learn from the Old Testament about social justice and about the liberating powers of God, but, while effective political action comes from having effective political power, the Christ whom Paul acclaims as the manifestation of the power of God is the crucified Christ, the one who is wholly deprived of power as the world understands it.

Reflection

Lord, help us to discover how power and powerlessness may be reconciled, so that we may continue to journey with you in new and transfiguring ways.

Andrew Jones

Hebrews: Jesus our great high priest

Traditionally Hebrews has been seen as a letter to Jewish believers who were in danger of returning to their Jewish practices rather than remaining faithful to Christ. More recently it has been argued that it may have been a mixed audience who received this letter.

Here, we will assume that it was addressed to both Jewish and Gentile believers. Some of them were struggling because of the way they were regarded by the rest of society. Their lifestyle and newfound values put these early Christians outside the accepted ways of being citizens at that time. Humiliation, rejection and marginalisation were tempting some to abandon their commitment to Jesus altogether.

The author held before them the supreme worth of the one in whom they had first trusted, showing them, in the rhetorical style of the day, that if one thing was good, Jesus was far better. Two courses of action lay open: to remain committed to the Christian confession of faith and hope or to turn 'away from the living God' (Hebrews 2:12).

By comparing Jesus with earlier mediators recorded in the scriptures, the author shows the wonderful advantages of continuing in the faith and so highlights the folly of shrinking back or drifting away. Just as the commander of an army would need to exhort his troops before battle, as there would be those who were ready for action as well as those who were full of fear and misgivings, the latter kind of Christians needed an injection of courage and renewal of their vision to keep going.

Despite the decline of respect for Christian faith in our own times, we need not fear being dragged from our beds and punished for following Jesus. We may have Jesus and wealth, status and safety all at the same time and perhaps this is the point at which we need to pay attention. Hebrews challenges us to think again about what discipleship means in our culture and offers us strategies to help us grow faithful communities of committed believers. Hebrews reminds us of the honour of being made members of God's family and the welcome that awaits believers in the kingdom of heaven. In this letter, Jesus is central throughout and we are shown how to make that true in our lives today.

Liz Hoare

Majesty on high

Long ago God spoke to our ancestors in many and various ways by the prophets, but in these last days he has spoken to us by a Son, whom he appointed heir of all things, through whom he also created the worlds. He is the reflection of God's glory and the exact imprint of God's very being, and he sustains all things by his powerful word. When he had made purification for sins, he sat down at the right hand of the Majesty on high, having become as much superior to angels as the name he has inherited is more excellent than theirs.

I am writing this on Ascension Day, when we celebrate the joyful and triumphant climax of the Easter story: Jesus is risen, ascended and glorified. The writer begins his letter at this same point of climax, with Jesus, the exact imprint of God himself, now seated at his right hand in the heavens. All attention is focused on God's word as spoken through his Son. By beginning here, we are orientated right from the start according to a different worldview.

The writer begins with the evocative words, 'Long ago' (v. 1), inviting us to reflect on the story of God's dealings with his world. By referring to the 'many and various ways' (v. 1) that God has spoken to his people in the past, including prophets and even angels (see the rest of chapter 1, especially v. 14), the writer is beginning his technique of demonstrating how everything in the Old Testament has been leading towards this final revelation of God. It speaks of his activity before the coming of the Lord Jesus and also his ministry after his ascension into the heavenly realm. It is as if all the pieces of a huge jigsaw have been put in place to reveal the greatness of the Lord Jesus Christ. In him, we have the final picture of what God is doing in history. It is a picture of an unshakeable realm (12:28), in which every believer may have complete confidence because of Jesus, who has gone there before us.

Prayer

O Lord, our Lord, how excellent is your name in all the earth. Amen
(Psalm 8:1, NKJV)

LIZ HOARE

No room for ambiguity

> Therefore we must pay greater attention to what we have heard, so that we do not drift away from it. For if the message declared through angels was valid, and every transgression or disobedience received a just penalty, how can we escape if we neglect so great a salvation?

This is not a rhetorical question but one that lies at the heart of the writer's concern for the recipients of this letter. If everything he has just written about Jesus is true—and it has been properly attested by such great and reliable authorities such as prophets and angels—it is essential that we do not disregard it.

The command to 'pay… attention' (v. 1) leaves no room for ambiguity. To pay attention is to focus on something with the whole of your being, eyes, ears, heart and mind. Some things in life only come through careful and prolonged attention. I love watching birds, for example, but a lot of the time it is a case of patient and prolonged waiting with my attention fully engaged so as not to miss them. If we are involved in any kind of detailed work, be it mathematical, sewing, woodwork or listening, it is vital to remain engaged, paying careful attention to what is before us in the present.

The Christian life, which involves all of us, is no different. How do we pay attention to our salvation? The writer of this letter to the Hebrews turns to the Old Testament where many failures to pay attention to God's word are recorded. If these examples led to penalties, how much more serious will it be if we drift away from God's final revelation in Jesus, who is so much greater even than the angels? This may sound like a threat, but we will go on to discover the great and wonderful benefits of faith in Christ. We will see that it is utter folly to think that there is any truly valid alternative to holding firmly to our confidence in him. There is simply too much at stake to not pay close attention and stay the course.

Prayer

Lord Jesus, please help me to pay attention today to the grace I have received in you. Thank you for so great a salvation. Amen

LIZ HOARE

Beware drifting away

Take care, brothers and sisters, that none of you may have an evil, unbelieving heart that turns away from the living God. But exhort one another every day, as long as it is called 'today', so that none of you may be hardened by the deceitfulness of sin. For we have become partners of Christ, if only we hold our first confidence firm to the end.

In Hebrews 3:3, we are told that 'Jesus is worthy of more glory than Moses, just as the builder of a house has more honour than the house itself.' The writer is not saying, 'Forget Moses, he was no good.' Moses was, after all, a key figure of the Old Testament and the writer is using the scriptures to show how wonderful Jesus is and how worthy of wholehearted commitment. In fact, what he is saying is that, if Moses was great, Jesus is much greater still and, therefore, it is vital to trust him always. Just as those who were in the wilderness with Moses came to a bad end because they failed to trust God's promises, so giving up on Christ will mean that we forfeit all the benefits of salvation in him. What would make us do such a thing?

For the original hearers, it may well have been fear of the consequences of commitment to an alien and misunderstood religion. It was much easier to go with the flow and conform to society's norms. Most of us will have felt the pressure to do this at various times. What helps get us back on track so often is having the encouragement of others who share our faith and, hence, our outlook. It is vital that we both give and receive this encouragement.

As those early Christians saw their situation mirrored in the wilderness experience of Moses, so perhaps we may identify with theirs in turn and recognise afresh the value of belonging to our various church fellowships. As we meet together, we can exhort each other and build each other up in Christ. Drifting away is a subtle business (see v. 13) and we need to be constantly vigilant against it.

Prayer

Lord Jesus, help me to encourage someone in their faith today. Amen

LIZ HOARE

Promised rest

Therefore, while the promise of entering his rest is still open, let us take care that none of you should seem to have failed to reach it. For indeed the good news came to us just as to them; but the message they heard did not benefit them, because they were not united by faith with those who listened. For we who have believed enter that rest.

Chapter 4 is all about entering God's rest. In a frantic world where rest is scorned by those who want to get on and are ready to pay the price of ever-increasing activity, rest is an immediately counter-cultural concept. God's rest, however, is not just about having a day off every week, though that is a powerful statement in itself. It says that God, not me, is dictating the flow of time and the pattern of our days. It says that I can let go now and then and I do not have to be in control. All this is implicit in 'God's rest' as used here, but there is so much more to it than just that.

'Entering the rest' (v. 1) is concerned with entering God's realm—a realm beyond this world, an unshakeable kingdom where God reigns in glory. It is an image for the goal that every believer is aiming for: the salvation wrought for us (1:14), the glory we are being led towards (2:10), the better heavenly homeland (11:16) and the city that is to come (13:14). We are both entering it in the present time (4:3) and we are to strive earnestly to enter it in the future (4:11). It is as if we are standing on the threshold of the heavenly realm and need to keep on until we have finally crossed it. It is rather like saying, 'I have been saved', but at the same time saying, 'I will be saved.'

God's grace and our trust in him enable us to enter God's rest. We may be confident of this because Jesus, our great high priest, has already entered God's rest before us. What could help you to picture what experiencing God's rest would look like for you?

Reflection

'A sabbath rest still remains for the people of God' (Hebrews 4:9).

LIZ HOARE

The perfect advocate

Since, then, we have a great high priest who has passed through the heavens, Jesus, the Son of God, let us hold fast to our confession. For we do not have a high priest who is unable to sympathise with our weaknesses, but we have one who in every respect has been tested as we are, yet without sin. Let us therefore approach the throne of grace with boldness, so that we may receive mercy and find grace to help in time of need.

In the preceding few verses the image of the all-piercing, all-seeing word of God has reminded us of our naked vulnerability before him and now the writer brings to centre stage the pivot of what he wants us to grasp with all our heart and soul. It is Jesus, the living word of God, who took flesh and suffered (2:10, 14) and who alone can help us (2:18).

Have you ever been in a situation where you are dependent on an advocate who is prepared to speak up on your behalf? How important it is to be able to trust such a person and know that he or she understands your situation accurately so can represent you clearly and sympathetically. Similarly, the writer here repeats his assertion that Jesus knows what it is like to be in our situation (compare 2:18 and 5:2), so as to emphasise the point that he is the perfect mediator. This is because he is also perfect, like God himself, before whom he stands on our behalf.

In asking us to hold fast to our confession, the writer means us to hold on to the new worldview with all its present benefits and future hopes that Christ has opened up for us through his death and resurrection. His chief gift to human beings is to go before us through the heavens to give us access to God himself. We can be confident before him because he is one of us and therefore understands us, yet is without sin. What other response can there be to him but total and lasting devotion?

Prayer

In prayer, let us approach the throne of grace with confidence today.

LIZ HOARE

Keeping going

So also Christ did not glorify himself in becoming a high priest, but was appointed by the one who said to him, 'You are my Son, today I have begotten you'; as he says also in another place, 'You are a priest forever, according to the order of Melchizedek.'

Having focused on Jesus, our great high priest, the writer now elaborates and draws out the implications of this for believers. Hebrews 4:14—10:18 forms the central exposition of an extended sermon about Jesus' priesthood and deserves to be read in full. Today's passage describes the relationship between God the Father and the Son. The important point is that Jesus was not a self-appointed high priest, but was chosen directly by God. This is where his authority lies. Jesus never sought glory for himself, as we know from the hymn in Philippians 2.

Having stated his divine authority, much is then made of Jesus' humanity—'Although he was a Son' (Hebrews 5:8)—and the writer regrets not being able to say even more because of the immaturity of his hearers (vv. 11–14). If Christ has been made perfect (or reached his goal), the recipients of this sermon clearly have not. Their immaturity is exposed and they are exhorted to keep going towards their appointed goal and, thus, grow up.

There are certainly some difficult passages in Hebrews and we have to work hard to grasp their original meaning. What do you do when you encounter Bible passages that seem difficult to understand? The writer talks about being trained through practice and the importance of not giving up. Just as we have the example of Jesus before us, who persevered in obedience through prayer, so we also have the promises that await us as we walk by faith in him.

Prayer

O God, who has prepared for those who love you such good things as pass our understanding: pour into our hearts such love towards you that we, loving you in all things and above all things, may obtain your promises which exceed all we can desire; through Jesus Christ our Lord who lives and reigns with you. Amen

Collect for the 6th Sunday after Trinity, *Common Worship*
LIZ HOARE

An anchor for the soul

> We have this hope, a sure and steadfast anchor of the soul, a hope that enters the inner shrine behind the curtain, where Jesus, a forerunner on our behalf, has entered, having become a high priest forever according to the order of Melchizedek.

Nautical imagery recurs in Hebrews and describes well the importance placed on perseverance in adversity. 'Hold fast,' the writer says (4:14); 'do not drift away' (2:1). Here, the image of the anchor of the soul emphasises the firm and constant quality of Christian hope that rests securely in Jesus. The anchor is the fixed point in the life of Christians that keeps us from drifting away. It holds us firmly when life's storms come and it keeps us connected to the source of our salvation.

The picture changes quickly, to the inner shrine of the temple—something familiar to the original hearers but perhaps strange to us. The inmost part of the temple was the most holy and was screened from view by a thick curtain (according to Mark 15:38, this was the curtain that was torn in two when Jesus died). No one could go there except for the high priest and even he was allowed in just once a year. What a shocking thing, then, to imagine free and open access to it for ordinary folk! We are encouraged to hold on to this expectation of ready access because Jesus has gone there before us as the forerunner (the word is a military one, denoting a scout who goes ahead of the main body of the army to lead them).

The two pictures, one of hope as an anchor and the other of the inner shrine of the temple, are connected to each other by the lifeline of hope. This hope has already entered where Jesus has gone and the expectation is that many will follow after him. These verses are both a statement of truth and an encouragement to keep going. Which facet speaks to you today?

Reflection

We have an anchor that keeps the soul steadfast and sure while the billows roll, fastened to the rock which cannot move, grounded firm and deep in the Saviour's love.

Priscilla Owens, 1882

LIZ HOARE

Supreme advocate

> [Jesus] holds his priesthood permanently, because he continues
> forever. Consequently he is able for all time to save those who
> approach God through him, since he always lives to make inter-
> cession for them.

Having an advocate when we need someone to speak up for us can be
very reassuring in many difficult and delicate human situations.
Knowing that we have an advocate in *heaven* to speak up for us is an
astounding truth that lies at the heart of the gospel. It completely trans-
forms the way we approach prayer if we know that the same Jesus who
taught us to say, 'Our Father in heaven' is in the Father's presence, praying for us now. Even more than this, we can be confident that we are
acceptable in God's sight because of Jesus' priestly ministry of intercession. God's favour towards us is dependent on the fact that Jesus, who
has died, is risen and has ascended into heaven, now intercedes for us.

We rest our confidence on the truth of the resurrection. Raising Jesus
from the dead was not only God's vindication of his self-offering of
himself on behalf of the sins of the world but also, having ascended to
the heavenly realm, Jesus, even now, continues to act on our behalf. The
resurrection not only underpins the whole argument of Hebrews but
also provides the guarantee that Jesus continues to act on our behalf in
the heavenly realm.

When we are tempted to give up or we are overwhelmed by a sense
of our own sinfulness, the truths contained in these verses will help to
transform our perception of the true situation, which is what really matters. The words 'permanently' and 'continues forever' lift us out of a
world that will pass away and into one where Jesus remains constant in
his priestly ministry. He is the foundation of our security; we do not
need any other intermediary before God to speak on our behalf. Hebrews
is urgent in its intention to help us to lift our eyes to see this new reality.
God's promises cannot fail because Jesus is their guarantor.

Prayer

*Lord Jesus, great high priest, thank you for your faithful intercession
for me today.*

LIZ HOARE

Once for all

Unlike the other high priests, he has no need to offer sacrifices day after day, first for his own sins, and then for those of the people; this he did once for all when he offered himself.

The thrust of chapters 7 and 8 is that of showing Jesus to be the most qualified mediator, which the world requires to be right with God. Why does the writer spend so much time comparing and contrasting the priestly work of Jesus with the Old Testament law when he could simply say that the old has passed away, now that Jesus has come? One of the things he achieves by such detailed analysis of the old priesthood is to demonstrate the surpassing value of Jesus' priestly work and its ongoing worth. 'This is how people used to approach God in previous times,' he is saying, 'but now in these last days you may approach him like this.'

If we think for a moment of the way we are tempted to rely on things other than God—status, material things, effort and so on—these can be words for us too. So, in chapter 7, the writer explains the priesthood of the mysterious Melchizedek, who is a 'type' or forerunner of Christ. In other words, he has many qualities that we see much more clearly in Christ himself. Melchizedek was greater than Abraham, yet Jesus is much greater still.

Today's verse shows the implications for us today. Jesus' mediation is superior in every way to that of the old priesthood, while Melchizedek is but a pale shadow of the reality of Jesus' self-offering. Jesus is 'holy, blameless, undefiled' (v. 26). If we recall the earlier chapters where his solidarity with sinners is stressed, here we have the essential difference demonstrated: Jesus 'has been made perfect forever' (v. 28). Being put right with God is impossible without the self-offering of the Lord Jesus. And all this rests on God's own promises (v. 28), on which we can rely absolutely.

Reflection

Spend some time today pondering the self-giving of Jesus and what difference that makes in how you approach the almighty God, how you regard yourself and others and how you live your life day by day.

LIZ HOARE

The very best qualified

Now the main point in what we are saying is this: we have such a high priest, one who is seated at the right hand of the throne of the Majesty in the heavens, a minister in the sanctuary and the true tent that the Lord, and not any mortal, has set up.

Here we see the same Jesus, who knows what it is like to be tempted as a human being, now exalted beyond every creature either on earth or in heaven, seated at God's right hand in the eternal realm. Here the writer draws on Psalm 110, which he has already referred to earlier in his letter, in order to show that Jesus is appointed as a priest by God and to reiterate the place he is given in the heavenly realm (compare Psalm 110:1, 4). He wants us to see that we have the best-qualified priest in every respect to come before God on our behalf. Up to this point we have had to rely on a priesthood set up by human means, albeit with God's authority, which could not escape the inevitability of continually having to make sacrifices for human sin (Hebrews 8:3). Since Jesus was appointed by God and not by human beings, we can be sure that his priesthood is of a different order altogether.

The following chapter will explain what is meant by the heavenly sanctuary and the heavenly priesthood of Jesus. His presence at the right hand of God is the basis on which Christians have the confidence to expect to be made perfect as we trust in a better hope (7:11, 19). Why, having discovered the very best, would anyone choose to return to something inferior? We, like the Christians to whom this letter was originally addressed, may have the confidence to approach God's throne anywhere, at any time, in any state of mind and know that there is a high priest who continues to live at God's right hand and intercede on our behalf.

Prayer

Lord Jesus, you reign on high and I worship you today, praising and thanking you for your supreme sacrifice on the cross for me.

LIZ HOARE

The value of faith

Now faith is the assurance of things hoped for, the conviction of things not seen. Indeed, by faith our ancestors received approval. By faith we understand that the worlds were prepared by the word of God, so that what is seen was made from things that are not visible... By faith Noah, warned by God about events as yet unseen... built an ark to save his household... By faith Abraham obeyed when he was called to set out for a place that he was to receive as an inheritance; and he set out, not knowing where he was going.

Are there people in your life who have shown you in some special way the value of living a life of faith? For the original audience of this letter, Noah, Abraham, Moses and others were proof that God honoured those whose lives showed faith in his promises.

They did not have the example of Jesus before them, but they looked forward to his coming and lived out their lives in the light of God's promises. They kept going in faith, sometimes in the face of ridicule, being misunderstood and worse (vv. 36–38). Their lives continue to set us examples of faith and are worth studying closely, but, first (v. 3), the writer reminds us it requires faith to trust that God made the world we know and inhabit, so every day involves faith of a kind.

Faith becomes Christian when its object of trust is Jesus. Yet, we too have to live the kind of faith that our Old Testament ancestors lived because we do not yet see all things restored in Christ.

The writer previously discussed the hope that we have in Jesus, who, as our supreme high priest, entered the inner shrine once and for all on our behalf (6:19–20) and this is the basis of our faith now. It is a hope that is anchored in the heavenly realm and, although we cannot see it, we may have absolute confidence in it. Faith builds on the firm foundation of hope.

Reflection

Ask God to encourage you in your faith today and look for ways to be an encouragement to someone else.

LIZ HOARE

Running the race

> Therefore... let us also lay aside every weight and the sin that clings so closely, and let us run with perseverance the race that is set before us, looking to Jesus the pioneer and perfecter of our faith, who for the sake of the joy that was set before him endured the cross, disregarding its shame, and has taken his seat at the right hand of the throne of God.

The athletic imagery here exhorts us to turn discouragement into perseverance as we press on towards the ultimate prize awaiting us. The example of Jesus captures the essence of the previous catalogue of Old Testament characters who exemplified faith in the centuries before his coming. His life provides an overarching pattern for believers, the climax of the catalogue of heroes of faith and our supreme example: 'the pioneer and perfecter of our faith' (v. 2).

Hebrews acknowledges that following Jesus may be hard. Like the Old Testament exemplars of faith, we, too, have to continue to trust on days when it seems hard to do so, as well as when we catch glimpses of God's glorious kingdom. Verse 1 exhorts us to throw off 'every weight' that hampers our participation in the race. For the original audience, this referred to reputation, physical safety and material wealth (10:32–34). We may recognise some of these hindrances in our own lives, perhaps especially the lure of material prosperity. Staying the course also meant turning away from sin (12:1).

As in any race, we grow weary and need help to keep going. The key to doing so is to keep on 'looking to Jesus' (v. 2). Even he was required to trust that God was working his purposes out as he faced the cross. He did so by focusing on the 'joy that was set before him' (v. 2). Thus, Jesus is both our supreme example and also the means by which we are to live by faith and keep on doing so in all circumstances. As we learn to practise the presence of God, we will grow increasingly attentive to the presence of Jesus with us, encouraging and enabling us to go on.

Prayer

Lord Jesus, make your presence known to me from the beginning of this day till its ending. Amen

LIZ HOARE

Heavenly city

But you have come to Mount Zion and to the city of the living God, the heavenly Jerusalem, and to innumerable angels in festal gathering… and to God the judge of all, and to the spirits of the righteous made perfect, and to Jesus, the mediator of a new covenant.

The author piles on the images that lead to a picture of triumph in the heavenly realm. While hymns of previous generations loved to utilise 'the language of Zion', we are less comfortable with it in case we seem too other-worldly. Hebrews, however, has been encouraging us all along to focus on the eternal reality for which God is preparing us. Through the work of Jesus, we are being made ready to take our place as citizens in the city of God. The previous verses contrast the way God had formerly been approached in fear and trepidation (vv. 18–21) with the confident and celebratory way we are invited to do so through Jesus (vv. 22–24). Exodus 19 and Deuteronomy 4 provide the background for the old way that people sought to draw near to God and highlight all the more clearly the wonderful privilege it now is to approach freely.

Membership of this eternal city must have been a huge encouragement for the early Christians. We, in our more comfortable setting, may need to work harder to connect with this vision. The writer is constantly at pains to exhort us to live well here so that we may be prepared for living in God's eternal kingdom. This will impinge on the choices we make, the desires we allow to govern our lifestyles, the company we keep and so on. Holding before us the 'surpassing value of knowing Christ' (Philippians 3:8), we may find ourselves empowered to live faithfully in this world and be ready for all that is to come. One way to regularly remind ourselves of this is to participate in the Lord's Supper.

Reflection

Therefore with angels and archangels and with all the company of heaven, we praise and magnify your glorious name, evermore praising you and saying, Holy, holy, holy Lord God of hosts: heaven and earth are full of your glory.

Prayer of Thanksgiving in the service of Holy Communion

LIZ HOARE

A response of gratitude

Therefore, since we are receiving a kingdom that cannot be shaken, let us give thanks, by which we offer to God an acceptable worship with reverence and awe; for indeed our God is a consuming fire.

Throughout Hebrews, the writer has stressed that the present world is not permanent (1:10–12). God will shake not only the earth but also the heavens, and remove them (12:26). The tottering of so many economies in recent years has brought home the fragility of security based on a material world. Christians, however, having learned to see beyond the immediate to what is as yet unseen, need not fear because we are destined to inhabit a realm that cannot be shaken. This privilege, with all the accompanying benefits of God's favour, was won for us through Jesus' costly mediation. Gratitude is the only appropriate response.

The ancient world understood gratitude towards a benefactor as an obligation. It involved giving honour to the benefactor and exercising absolute loyalty to them. It also involved seeking opportunities to serve. Our own society also understands the role of gratitude, although we are often depicted as ungrateful people who are demanding of our rights and self-centred in our attitudes. When we treat our church fellowships in a consumerist fashion, we allow these traits to infiltrate the body of Christ. Being grateful for what we have, rather than lamenting what we do not have, shifts our underlying focus. As the passage here states, our worship is affected by our gratitude or lack of it.

As if to underline the centrality of gratitude to the Christian life, the writer reminds us that 'our God is a consuming fire' (v. 29). Such a stern reminder highlights that we cannot treat the wonderful benefits wrought for us through Jesus' self-sacrifice thoughtlessly or ungratefully without risking grave consequences.

Prayer

Thank you, Lord Jesus Christ, for all the benefits you have given me, for all the pains and insults you have borne for me. O most merciful redeemer, friend and brother, may I know you more clearly, love you more dearly and follow you more nearly, day by day.

Richard, Bishop of Chichester, 1197–1253

LIZ HOARE

137

Steadfast and true

Jesus Christ is the same yesterday and today and forever.

Gratitude towards God for all he has bestowed on us deepens our awareness of those benefits and arouses in us an appropriate response back to him. Like a beautiful circle dance, we walk in the awareness of receiving from God and returning thanks to him through our worship and service and our sharing of what he has given us with one another. At the heart of the circle is Jesus himself, the faithful constant mediator.

It was Jesus' reliability that enabled the original hearers to remain firm and every reader of this text since must have drawn strength and assurance from its all-encompassing steadfastness. As exemplified by the anchor imagery in chapter 6, Jesus' trustworthiness stands firm throughout eternity. It is because of Jesus' steadfastness that we can remain steadfast in our turn and not be 'carried away' by the pressures of our daily lives. Thus, on either side of this central fixed point, we are directed to live lives that bring honour to our Lord and Saviour.

The author fleshes out the more general command to 'do good' in the early verses where exercising brotherly and sisterly love and showing hospitality (13:1–3) are followed by cautions regarding behaviour that might undermine the body of believers (vv. 4–6). We are to discover more of Jesus' faithfulness and reliability by playing our part in helping to grow a faithful and trustworthy body of believers.

Being reminded once again of the privilege of being identified with Jesus, we are to offer sacrifices of praise and good deeds. As we worship him, spread abroad his name and look out for one another, we live in a way that is pleasing to God. Our behaviour should extend beyond how we treat our fellow believers to how we behave as citizens in this world (v. 17), and and we should do it joyfully. There are real challenges for every believer in these verses, all arising out of the central confession of faith in an absolutely reliable saviour.

Prayer
Give thanks for the way Jesus has been faithful to you in the past and entrust yourself to him afresh for today and tomorrow.

LIZ HOARE

Supporting Messy Church with a gift in your will

For many charities, income from legacies is crucial in enabling them to plan ahead, and often provides the funding to develop new projects. Legacies make a significant difference to the ability of charities to achieve their purpose. In just this way, a legacy to support BRF's ministry would make a huge difference.

One of the fastest growing areas of BRF is its Messy Church ministry (www.messychurch.org.uk). Messy Church is a form of church focused on building relationships, engaging with people outside the usual church context and building a Christ-centred community. Messy Church gives families and all age groups an opportunity to be together and is a congregation in its own right. In addition, it is being delivered in a variety of different contexts in local communities, including care homes, prisons, inner cities, schools and rural areas. Week by week we are seeing new Messy Churches starting up across the UK and around the globe, across all major Christian denominations. A conservative estimate is that over 250,000 people are attending Messy Church each month.

Throughout its history, BRF's ministry has been enabled thanks to the generosity of those who have shared its vision and supported its work, both by giving during their lifetime and also through legacy gifts.

A legacy gift would help fund the development and sustainability of BRF's Messy Church ministry into the future. We hope you may consider a legacy gift to help us continue to take this work forward in the decades to come.

For further information about making a gift to BRF in your will or to discuss how a specific bequest could be used to develop our ministry, please contact Sophie Aldred (Head of Fundraising) or Richard Fisher (Chief Executive) by email at fundraising@brf.org.uk or by phone on 01865 319700.

This page is intentionally left blank.

The BRF

Magazine

Celebrating 25 years of ministry

Richard Fisher

In October 1988, Richard Fisher, BRF's Chief Executive, joined BRF. We asked him to reflect on the past 25 years.

What led you to work for BRF?

I was looking for something to do for a year between completing my university degree and going off to theological college. A friend mentioned that BRF was considering appointing a Field Officer for a one-year project; it sounded interesting so I applied and got the job. It was a great privilege to travel the length and breadth of the UK, introducing the work of BRF to some and reintroducing it to others—and that 'year off' has turned into 25 so far…

What was your first day like?

I'm not sure I recall my actual first day, but I remember that within a week of joining BRF I was manning the stand on my own at the Christian Resources Exhibition in Manchester. I'd never heard of BRF before I applied for the job and suddenly there I was, promoting BRF's publications at a three-day exhibition. That was a steep learning curve!

When BRF moved from London to Oxford in 1991, you became Chief Executive. What vision did you have for the organisation then?

I felt strongly, as others before me had done, that BRF was much more than just another Christian publisher. I wanted people to think of BRF more as a 'movement' seeking to resource the spiritual life and growth of individuals and congregations. I was asked in 1993 to set out a strategy for taking BRF forward and, while preparing this, I read all the minute books of BRF Trustee meetings dating back to 1922, when BRF started in St Matthew's Church, Brixton. I came to realise that what I thought was my fresh vision for BRF was, in fact, a rediscovery of the original vision of its founder, Canon Leslie Mannering.

What have been some of the highlights for you in the past 25 years?

There have been many! The establishment and growth of Barnabas Children's Ministry; the launch of Foundations21 as the first online discipleship resource of its kind, and then, more recently, being the first in the UK to make our Bible reading notes available as apps for iPhones and iPads; Messy Church and Who Let The Dads Out? becoming part of BRF and growing from local church initiatives to national (and, in the case of Messy Church, international) movements. Then there's been the thrill of seeing individual books occasionally published in unexpected languages—Arabic, Romanian, Ukrainian, Chinese, Afrikaans—and the interest that was generated in the secular media by our publication of *The Bible in Cockney*.

There have also been many memorable events—BRF's service of thanksgiving in Westminster Abbey in 1997, taking part in the pageants to mark The Queen Mother's 90th and 100th birthdays, and a BRF reception at Lambeth Palace in 2007 stand out as particular highlights.

BRF has expanded significantly in the past years. What factors do you believe have contributed to this growth?

Without doubt, BRF's greatest asset is its staff team, and I never cease to marvel at the way in which, so often, God has brought the right person to us at the right time. BRF has evolved organically over the years, often in ways that have taken us by surprise. I have no doubt that God has a plan for BRF and it's up to us to respond to the opportunities he has given to us. Looking back, one thing has often seemed to lead to another in the way BRF's ministries have developed.

We never thought, when we published the first book under our newly launched Barnabas children's imprint back in 1995, that this would lead to what has become Barnabas Children's Ministry, helping churches, primary schools and families to explore Christianity and the Bible. We never thought, when Lucy Moore (then a member of our Barnabas staff team) first told us back in 2005 about an initiative she and her husband had started in their church to reach out to their local community, that this would lead to Messy Church becoming a core ministry of BRF that, within only a few years, would extend not just throughout the UK but to numerous countries overseas as well. We first came across Who Let The Dads Out? in early 2010. We recognised that there were numerous points of connection between their vision to engage with fathers and their young children and what we were doing with both Messy Church and Barnabas Children's Ministry. None of us had any idea that, just three years later, we would announce that Who Let The Dads Out? had become part of BRF. And when two people I'd never met before asked to come and see me in September 2000 to talk about an idea for a new discipleship resource, little did we realise that this would be the start of a journey that would lead, more than six years later, to the launch of Foundations21.

In 2002, the BRF Council of Trustees approved a statement of purpose—'resourcing your spiritual journey'—which sums up what BRF is about. Everything we do relates to this purpose. Although our core ministries may, at first sight, seem to be quite different from one another, they complement and add value to one another in many ways. It really does all fit together and therein lies one of our main strengths.

There are two other very significant factors I must mention as well. One is the fantastic group of Trustees that we have at BRF, whose support, wisdom and encouragement have been key to our ability to take up the opportunities we have been given. The other is the trusts, churches and individuals whose financial support has made all the development possible. I am constantly amazed and humbled by their generosity towards BRF.

What Bible verse resonates with you most at the moment?

Jeremiah 29:11 is a verse that has meant a great deal to me for over 30 years now: '"For I know the plans I have for you," declares the Lord, "plans to prosper you and not to harm you, plans to give you a hope and a future."'

Looking ahead, what is your vision for BRF in the next few years and your ministry within the organisation?

My vision is for BRF to continue enabling, equipping and resourcing others, both in their ministries/roles and in their own personal journeys of faith and discipleship. I don't want to make them dependent on BRF, but rather to help them to grow and to discover and be able to exercise their own gifts. I hope we'll continue to be flexible and responsive to whatever new opportunities God gives us. I believe he still has work for me to do at BRF and I rather suspect that what started as a 'year off' could possibly turn out to be a life's work. But only God knows the answer to that!

A Good Childhood

Jim Davis

A Good Childhood by Liz Baddaley (Barnabas for Children) provides seven Bible studies for church groups, based on themes from the results of the Good Childhood Inquiry: values, inequality, family, well-being, friends, lifestyle and learning.

The Children's Society was established by Edward Rudolf in 1881. Rudolf, a Sunday school teacher, became concerned about the welfare of the children in his class, so he decided to find out about their home lives. What he found in the cramped, poverty-stricken streets of Victorian London led him to put his Christian faith into action, shaping the rest of his life and the lives of thousands of children. The basis of his action was to create a family environment for children devoid of such experience, where love could be expressed and freely given. More than 130 years later, the need to understand what is happening in children's lives and respond on the basis of love has not changed.

The Good Childhood Inquiry commissioned by The Children's Society was prompted by a desire to understand better what affects children in the UK in the 21st century and what adults need to do in order to ensure that every child has the opportunity to experience not just a 'good enough' childhood but one that is as good as we would want for our own children. The Inquiry published its findings in 2009, after the independent panel of experts drawn together by The Children's Society had scrutinised thousands of statements from children and from the research of academics all over the world. The recommendations were multiple, but one conclusion stood tall and prominent. The panel concluded that British society needed to be based on the law of love, that all children needed to grow up experiencing unconditional love and that love should be the foundation of all our interaction with children.

Since then, we have produced other studies into children's well-being, the experiences of young people running away from home, and the needs of children in poverty—all as a continuing exploration of what really happens in children's lives and how adults need to respond. Since the publication of the Good Childhood Inquiry report, I have listened to and spoken with thousands of children up and down the country. I have been into inner cities, affluent towns and small isolated villages; I have listened to troubled teenagers, contented toddlers, young asylum seekers and children with disabilities. I have spoken with young people who are passionate about their faith and with those who sneer at the notion of God. I wanted to hear their stories and ideas about life, to gain a better understanding of them and their experience of the world.

In all of that experience, I have been constantly in awe of how much children and young people have to say. As adults, we assume that young people grunt their way through adolescence and that, as we grow older, we will inevitably understand less of what children have to say, as they become more and more distant from us. I have not found that to be true. Children have a lot to say and they want the opportunity to say it to us and to be certain that we are listening.

In all that I have heard, one message emerges. It is strident, it is consistent and it is expressed by some as something they wish for and by others as something they are grateful for. Children value love above all other things. They recognise love as the foundation of a good childhood, as something that gives meaning to life and something that all are entitled to. Furthermore, they express love as something given unconditionally. Perhaps it is best summed up in the words of a five-year-old who told me that she thought love meant 'being cuddled even if I have been a little bit naughty'. Being held close, protected, provided for, forgiven and restored even when such actions are not deserved or when they are resisted—that is what children recognise as love. The consequences of unconditional love are not lost on children. They know how difficult it can be to forgive and to seek restoration for a broken relationship; they struggle through the complexities and messiness of their own friendships; and they look to us to model how it is done.

Children look at the way we adults relate to each other, how we treat each other and how we talk about each other. What they see and hear as children runs deep. If we want children to experience love as it should be, if we want them to grasp its meaning and act in ways that express love, then they need to see it in action. We need to love one another.

Jim Davis MBE has worked for The Children's Society for 29 years. His current role as Good Childhood Advisor aims to support a positive change in public attitudes toward children and young people. Jim was a panel member of The Good Childhood® Inquiry.

To order a copy of A Good Childhood, *please turn to the order form on page 155 or visit www.brfonline.org.uk.*

Recommended reading

Kevin Ball

One of the joys of writing this section of the BRF Magazine is to know that, for many of you, these reviews are valued as a source for discovering good books. This time we have two new authors for BRF who have already thrilled readers with their earlier books published elsewhere.

Journalist Carmel Thomason's first book, the bestselling *Every Moment Counts: A life of Mary Butterwick*, was listed in the Top 10 Christian books by *Church Times*, Amazon and WHSmith. Carmel's latest book, *Against the Odds*, presents the true stories of eight people who have uncovered the strength and peace that freely offering forgiveness can bring in some of the most extreme situations.

If you enjoy reading about the Celtic church, Ray Simpson is a name you will recognise. In his latest book, *Hilda of Whitby*, Ray takes us to the seventh century AD to meet a highly influential, if little-known woman who became a significant figure in the development of the infant British church amid the chaos of the Anglo-Saxon years.

Also in the reviews that follow are a new devotional commentary on the Psalms, a resource for anyone looking for new preaching or group study ideas, and a book intriguingly entitled *Edible Bible Crafts*. This is just a taste (yes, pun intended!) of our summer publications for 2014.

To order, please complete the order form at the back of your Bible reading notes, visit www.brfonline.org.uk or ring our Customer Service team on 01865 319700.

You can also receive regular BRF book information, offers and ministry news direct into your inbox by signing up at www.brfonline.org.uk/enews-signup/

Against the Odds
True stories of healing and forgiveness
Carmel Thomason

'The old law of an eye for an eye leaves everybody blind' (Martin Luther King Jr.)

The act of forgiveness doesn't sit easily with our natural desire for justice. If something happens that is perceived as unfair, there is something deep inside that demands the wrong to be made right. It is a call we recognise in ourselves, hear in conversations and see as an essential part of most news stories that stream from newspapers, radio and TV daily. Against this inner demand stands the instruction of Jesus to forgive not once but continually. How can we reconcile these two apparent extremes?

Carmel Thomason presents the testimonies of eight people who have more reason than most not to forgive and yet, in the darkest of situations, have discovered the release and peace that forgiveness brings.

The book is split into two parts. The testimonies in Part 1 come from stories of war, crime and terrorism, events that most of us will not have to experience. They remind us all, however, that behind the breaking news story are real people, deeply hurt by events from which they need to find a way to rebuild and move on.

In Part 2, Carmel presents testimonies of everyday stories of forgiveness, which challenge us to ask, 'Are we keeping a record of rights and wrongs against those we love or have loved, or against ourselves, which is harming us not only as human beings but also as Christians?'

In both parts of the book, after each testimony is a short reflection on the story, drawing out its implications for understanding forgiveness. Questions are also provided for reading groups.

pb, 978 1 84101 739 6, £8.99

The Psalms
A commentary for reflection and prayer
Henry Wansbrough

A compilation of the daily readings on the Psalms written by one of the UK's leading Catholic scholars, Henry Wansbrough OSB, for BRF's *Guidelines* Bible reading notes. The commentary, which covers all 150 psalms, draws on current biblical scholarship, providing insight into the background (historical, literary and cultural) of each psalm and illustrated from Henry's own years of living and working in the Middle East. The commentary is a helpful companion for personal devotion as well as for preaching.

pb, 978 1 84101 648 1, £8.99

Hilda of Whitby
A spirituality for now
Ray Simpson

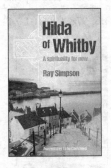

In the dark and turbulent centuries after the Roman occupation, which witnessed the invasion and colonisation of vast areas of the country by Anglo-Saxon tribes, the gospel light continued to shine across Britain through the witness of the monastic communities—known as 'villages of God'—that dotted the land.

One of the most remarkable figures of that period was Hilda of Whitby. Born and reared amid warring pagan tribes, through the influence of Celtic saints and scholars she became not only the founding abbess of Whitby monastery but also a dominant figure in the development of the British church.

Ray Simpson, international speaker, author and founding Guardian of the Community of Aidan and Hilda, investigates the drama of Hilda's life and ministry and presents the spiritual lessons we can draw for Christian life and leadership today. Published to coincide with the 1400th anniversary of Hilda's birth.

pb, 978 1 84101 728 0, £7.99

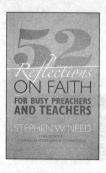

52 Reflections on Faith for Busy Preachers and Teachers
From the Sinai summits to the Emmaus road
Stephen W. Need

Formerly a New Testament Studies tutor and now a priest in Chelmsford Diocese, Stephen W. Need offers a wealth of personal inspiration for preachers as well as stimulating material for group study in these 52 reflections on selected stories from the Bible. He explores both biblical and theological dimensions and also makes connections with wider culture.

The book is split into two main sections: the first part provides reflections for the Sundays of the Christian year, from Advent to the feast of Christ the King, while the second part offers reflections that consider core aspects of Christian belief.

pb, 978 1 84101 743 3, £9.99

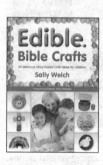

Edible Bible Crafts
64 delicious story-based craft ideas for children
Sally Welch

A range of edible crafts for 3- to 11-year-olds, covering twelve Old Testament and twelve New Testament stories and eight key festivals from the church year. Each unit gives the Bible story in a children's version, a short reflection on the passage, and both sweet and savoury recipe ideas. The recipes use readily available ingredients and equipment, require no cooking during the craft session and can be used in a variety of situations, including Sunday schools, midweek clubs and Messy Church events.

The book includes detailed information about set-up and preparation, tips on where to buy ingredients, and recipes to form the basis of the crafts.

pb, 978 0 85746 243 5, £11.99

To order copies of any of these books, please turn to the order form on page 155, or visit www.brfonline.org.uk.

As a Christian charity, BRF is involved in seven distinct yet complementary areas.

- **BRF** (www.brf.org.uk) resources adults for their spiritual journey through Bible reading notes, books and Quiet Days. BRF also provides the infrastructure that supports our other specialist ministries.
- **Foundations21** (www.foundations21.net) provides flexible and innovative ways for individuals and groups to explore their Christian faith and discipleship through a multimedia internet-based resource.
- **Messy Church** (www.messychurch.org.uk), led by Lucy Moore, enables churches all over the UK (and increasingly abroad) to reach children and adults beyond the fringes of the church.
- **Barnabas in Churches** (www.barnabasinchurches.org.uk) helps churches to support, resource and develop their children's ministry with the under-11s more effectively.
- **Barnabas in Schools** (www.barnabasinschools.org.uk) enables primary school children and teachers to explore Christianity creatively and bring the Bible alive within RE and Collective Worship.
- **Faith in Homes** (www.faithinhomes.org.uk) supports families to explore and live out the Christian faith at home.
- **Who Let The Dads Out** (www.wholetthedadsout.org) inspires churches to engage with dads and their pre-school children.

At the heart of BRF's ministry is a desire to equip adults and children for Christian living—helping them to read and understand the Bible, explore prayer and grow as disciples of Jesus. We need your help to make an impact on the local church, local schools and the wider community.

- You could support BRF's ministry with a one-off gift or regular donation (using the response form on page 153).
- You could consider making a bequest to BRF in your will.
- You could encourage your church to support BRF as part of your church's giving to home mission—perhaps focusing on a specific area of our ministry, or a particular member of our Barnabas team.
- Most important of all, you could support BRF with your prayers.

If you would like to discuss how a specific gift or bequest could be used in the development of our ministry, please phone 01865 319700 or email enquiries@brf.org.uk.

Whatever you can do or give, we thank you for your support.

Thank you for reading BRF Bible reading notes. BRF has been producing a variety of Bible reading notes for over 90 years, helping people all over the UK and the world connect with the Bible on a personal level every day.

Could you help us find other people who would enjoy our notes?

We produce a Bible Reading Resource Pack for church groups to use to encourage regular Bible reading.

This FREE pack contains:

- Samples of all BRF Bible reading notes.
- Our Resources for Personal Bible Reading catalogue, providing all you need to know about our Bible reading notes.
- A ready-to-use church magazine feature about BRF notes.
- Ready-made sermon and all-age service ideas to help your church into the Bible (ideal for Bible Sunday events).
- And much more!

How to order your FREE pack:

- Visit: www.biblereadingnotes.org.uk/request-a-bible-reading-resources-pack/
- Telephone: 01865 319700 between 9.15 and 17.30
- Post: Complete the form below and post to: Bible Reading Resource Pack, BRF, 15 The Chambers, Vineyard, Abingdon, OX14 3FE

Name _____

Address _____

_____

_____ Postcode _____

Telephone _____

Email _____

Please send me _____ Bible Reading Resources Pack(s)

This pack is produced free of charge for all UK addresses but, if you wish to offer a donation towards our costs, this would be appreciated. If you require a pack to be sent outside of the UK, please contact us for details of postage and packing charges. Tel: +44 1865 319700. Thank you.

BRF MINISTRY APPEAL RESPONSE FORM

I want to help BRF by funding some of its core ministries. Please use my gift for:

❏ Where most needed ❏ Barnabas Children's Ministry ❏ Foundations21

❏ Messy Church ❏ Who Let The Dads Out?

Please complete all relevant sections of this form and print clearly.

Title _____ First name/initials _____ Surname _____

Address _____

_____ Postcode _____

Telephone _____ Email _____

Regular giving

If you would like to give by standing order, please contact Debra McKnight (tel: 01235 462305; email debra.mcknight@brf.org.uk; write to BRF address).

If you would like to give by direct debit, please tick the box below and fill in details:

❏ I would like to make a regular gift of £ _____ per month / quarter / year (delete as appropriate) by Direct Debit. (Please complete the form on page 159.)

One-off donation

Please accept my special gift of

❏ £10 ❏ £50 ❏ £100 (other) £ _____ by

❏ Cheque / Charity Voucher payable to 'BRF'

❏ Visa / Mastercard / Charity Card

(delete as appropriate)

Name on card _____

Card no. ⬚⬚⬚⬚ ⬚⬚⬚⬚ ⬚⬚⬚⬚ ⬚⬚⬚⬚

Start date ⬚⬚⬚ Expiry date ⬚⬚⬚

Security code ⬚⬚⬚

Signature _____ Date _____

❏ I would like to give a legacy to BRF. Please send me further information.

If you would like to Gift Aid your donation, please fill in the form overleaf.

Please detach and send this completed form to: Debra McKnight, BRF, 15 The Chambers, Vineyard, Abingdon OX14 3FE. BRF is a Registered Charity (No.233280)

GIFT AID DECLARATION

Bible Reading Fellowship

Please treat as Gift Aid donations all qualifying gifts of money made
today ☐   in the past 4 years ☐   in the future ☐   (tick all that apply)

I confirm I have paid or will pay an amount of Income Tax and/or Capital Gains Tax for each tax year (6 April to 5 April) that is at least equal to the amount of tax that all the charities that I donate to will reclaim on my gifts for that tax year. I understand that other taxes such as VAT or Council Tax do not qualify. I understand the charity will reclaim 25p of tax on every £1 that I give on or after 6 April 2008.

Donor's details

Title _____ First name or initials _____ Surname _____

Full home address _____

_____

Postcode _____

Date _____

Signature _____

Please notify Bible Reading Fellowship if you:

- want to cancel this declaration
- change your name or home address
- no longer pay sufficient tax on your income and/or capital gains.

If you pay Income Tax at the higher or additional rate and want to receive the additional tax relief due to you, you must include all your Gift Aid donations on your Self-Assessment tax return or ask HM Revenue and Customs to adjust your tax code.

ND0214

BRF PUBLICATIONS ORDER FORM

Please send me the following book(s):

		Quantity	Price	Total
688 7	Creative Prayer Ideas (C. Daniel)	_____	£8.99	_____
728 0	Hilda of Whitby (R. Simpson)	_____	£7.99	_____
584 2	Transformed by the Beloved (D. Munoz)	_____	£6.99	_____
739 6	Against the Odds (C. Thomason)	_____	£8.99	_____
648 1	The Psalms (H. Wansbrough)	_____	£8.99	_____
743 3	52 Reflections for Busy Preachers (S.W. Need)	_____	£9.99	_____
146 9	A Good Childhood (L. Baddaley)	_____	£6.99	_____
163 6	Parenting Children for a Life of Purpose (R. Turner)	_____	£8.99	_____
243 5	Edible Bible Crafts (S. Welch)	_____	£11.99	_____

Total cost of books £ _____
Donation £ _____
Postage and packing £ _____
TOTAL £ _____

POSTAGE AND PACKING CHARGES				
order value	UK	Europe	Surface	Air Mail
£7.00 & under	£1.25	£3.00	£3.50	£5.50
£7.01–£30.00	£2.25	£5.50	£6.50	£10.00
Over £30.00	free	prices on request		

Please complete the payment details below and send with payment to: **BRF, 15 The Chambers, Vineyard, Abingdon OX14 3FE**

Name _____

Address _____

_____ Postcode _____

Tel _____ Email _____

Total enclosed £ _____ (cheques should be made payable to 'BRF')

Please charge my Visa ❑ Mastercard ❑ Switch card ❑ with £ _____

Card no: ☐☐☐☐ ☐☐☐☐ ☐☐☐☐ ☐☐☐☐ ☐☐☐☐

Expires ☐☐☐☐ Security code ☐☐☐

Issue no (Switch only) ☐☐☐☐

Signature (essential if paying by credit/Switch) _____

NEW DAYLIGHT INDIVIDUAL SUBSCRIPTIONS

❏ I would like to take out a subscription myself:

Your name _____

Your address _____

_____ Postcode _____

Tel _____ Email _____

Please send *New Daylight* beginning with the September 2014 / January 2015 / May 2015 issue: (delete as applicable)

(please tick box)	UK	SURFACE	AIR MAIL
NEW DAYLIGHT	❏ £15.99	❏ £23.25	❏ £25.50
NEW DAYLIGHT 3-year sub	❏ £40.50		
NEW DAYLIGHT DELUXE	❏ £19.80	❏ £30.75	❏ £36.75
NEW DAYLIGHT daily email only	❏ £12.75 (UK and overseas)		

Please complete the payment details below and send with appropriate payment to: **BRF, 15 The Chambers, Vineyard, Abingdon OX14 3FE**

Total enclosed £ _____ (cheques should be made payable to 'BRF')

Please charge my Visa ❏ Mastercard ❏ Switch card ❏ with £ _____

Card no: ☐☐☐☐ ☐☐☐☐ ☐☐☐☐ ☐☐☐☐ ☐☐☐☐

Expires ☐☐☐☐   Security code ☐☐☐

Issue no (Switch only) ☐☐☐☐

Signature (essential if paying by card) _____

To set up a direct debit, please also complete the form on page 159 and send it to BRF with this form.

BRF is a Registered Charity

ND0214

NEW DAYLIGHT GIFT SUBSCRIPTIONS

❏ I would like to give a gift subscription (please provide both names and addresses:

Your name _____

Your address _____

_____ Postcode _____

Tel _____ Email _____

Gift subscription name _____

Gift subscription address _____

_____ Postcode _____

Gift message (20 words max. or include your own gift card for the recipient)

_____

_____

Please send *New Daylight* beginning with the September 2014 / January 2015 / May 2015 issue: (delete as applicable)

(please tick box)	UK	SURFACE	AIR MAIL
NEW DAYLIGHT	❏ £15.99	❏ £23.25	❏ £25.50
NEW DAYLIGHT 3-year sub	❏ £40.50		
NEW DAYLIGHT DELUXE	❏ £19.80	❏ £30.75	❏ £36.75
NEW DAYLIGHT daily email only	❏ £12.75 (UK and overseas)		

Please complete the payment details below and send with appropriate payment to: **BRF, 15 The Chambers, Vineyard, Abingdon OX14 3FE**

Total enclosed £ _____ (cheques should be made payable to 'BRF')

Please charge my Visa ❏ Mastercard ❏ Switch card ❏ with £ _____

Card no: | | | | | | | | | | | | | | | | | |

Expires | | | | | Security code | | |

Issue no (Switch only) | | | |

Signature (essential if paying by card) _____

To set up a direct debit, please also complete the form on page 159 and send it to BRF with this form.

DIRECT DEBIT PAYMENTS

Now you can pay for your annual subscription to BRF notes using Direct Debit. You need only give your bank details once, and the payment is made automatically every year until you cancel it. If you would like to pay by Direct Debit, please use the form opposite, entering your BRF account number under 'Reference'.

You are fully covered by the Direct Debit Guarantee:

The Direct Debit Guarantee

- This Guarantee is offered by all banks and building societies that accept instructions to pay Direct Debits.
- If there are any changes to the amount, date or frequency of your Direct Debit, The Bible Reading Fellowship will notify you 10 working days in advance of your account being debited or as otherwise agreed. If you request The Bible Reading Fellowship to collect a payment, confirmation of the amount and date will be given to you at the time of the request.
- If an error is made in the payment of your Direct Debit, by The Bible Reading Fellowship or your bank or building society, you are entitled to a full and immediate refund of the amount paid from your bank or building society.
  - – If you receive a refund you are not entitled to, you must pay it back when The Bible Reading Fellowship asks you to.
- You can cancel a Direct Debit at any time by simply contacting your bank or building society. Written confirmation may be required. Please also notify us.

The Bible Reading Fellowship

Instruction to your bank or building society to pay by Direct Debit

Please fill in the whole form using a ballpoint pen and send to The Bible Reading Fellowship, 15 The Chambers, Vineyard, Abingdon OX14 3FE.

Service User Number:

5	5	8	2	2	9

Name and full postal address of your bank or building society

To: The Manager	Bank/Building Society
Address	
	Postcode

Name(s) of account holder(s)

Branch sort code	Bank/Building Society account number

Reference

Instruction to your Bank/Building Society

Please pay The Bible Reading Fellowship Direct Debits from the account detailed in this instruction, subject to the safeguards assured by the Direct Debit Guarantee.
I understand that this instruction may remain with The Bible Reading Fellowship and, if so, details will be passed electronically to my bank/building society.

Signature(s)
Date

Banks and Building Societies may not accept Direct Debit instructions for some types of account.

This page is intentionally left blank.